I've Got To Change

NIHIL OBSTAT
  Very Rev. John D. Byrnes, J.C.L., J.V.
  Censor of Books

IMPRIMATUR
  + Joseph V. Adamec, S.T.L, D.D.
  Bishop of Altoona-Johnstown

Hollidaysburg, 26 August 2009

The *Nihil Obstat* and *Imprimatur* are official declarations that a book or pamphlet is free of doctrinal or moral error. No implication is contained therein that those who have granted the *Nihil Obstat* and *Imprimatur* agree with the contents, opinions, or statements expressed.

I've Got To Change
Sean C. McVeigh

McVeigh Ministries Inc.
Pennsylvania

I've Got To Change

Copyright © 2009 by Sean C. McVeigh
McVeigh Ministries Inc.

All rights reserved. No part of this book may be used or reproduced by any means, graphic, electronic, or mechanical, including photocopying, recording, taping or by any information storage retrieval system without the written permission of the publisher except in the case of brief quotations embodied in critical articles and reviews.

McVeigh Ministries Inc. books may be ordered through booksellers or through:
McVeigh Ministries Inc.
P.O. Box 300
Lamar, PA 16848
www.CatholicGuestSpeaker.com

All of the Scripture references in this book were taken from the New American Bible Copyright © 1987 by Word Publishing Inc.

With the exception of the author and his cousin, every individual's name in this book has been changed to conceal their identity.

Editors–Anne Chavez, Jane McVeigh, Monsignor Anthony Little

ISBN: 978-0-9841011-0-8 (pbk)

Library of Congress Control Number: 2009905799

Printed in the United States of America
August 28, 2009

Contents

PART ONE—I Never Thought This Would Happen to Me 1
    METAL THUNDER 1
    AT THE HOSPITAL 8
    NEAR DEATH EXPERIENCE? 8
    THE SITUATION I NEVER WANTED TO BE IN 9
    PROVIDING A SAMPLE 10
    MY PARENTS 10
    THE PRIEST 11
    SURGERY, IS IT GOING TO HURT? 11
    DOCTORS REPORT 12
    SIDE EFFECTS 13
    FORMER BEST FRIEND 13
    WHAT HAPPENED TO THE OTHER GUYS IN THE CAR?
    14
    STOLEN HEART 15
    DON'T YOU WANT TO BEAT HIM UP? 15
    GOD'S GRACE 16
    WHEN CAN I GO HOME? 16

PART TWO—Out of the Hospital and Senior Year 18
    IF I WOULD HAVE DIED 18
    THIS CAME AS A SURPRISE 20
    CRUSHED 22
    FIRST DAY BACK 23

- NEXT TABLE OVER 24
- ONE MORE TRIAL 25
- APPLY YOURSELF 26
- GIRLFRIEND 26
- WHAT ARE MY MORAL CONVICTIONS? 28
- FOOLPROOF PLAN 29
- DIDN'T SEE IT COMING 32

PART THREE—The Beginning of My College Days 36
- FIRST SEMESTER AT PENN STATE 36
- UNEXPECTED WAKEUP CALL 38
- TURBULENT ENDING... 40
- SUMMER 42
- NO WAY! 44
- A MAJOR LIFE LESSON 45
- SMILE.. 46
- FINALLY! THIS IS THE ONE! 47
- DREADING A LONG DISTANCE RELATIONSHIP 48
- KICK IT 49
- FIRST SEMESTER, PHONE TIME 50
- TOE 51
- REVISITED 51
- ROUGH SEMESTER 53
- THE TRAGIC CALL... 56
- THE VIEWING 58
- GOD IS TALKING 58

COMFORTED	61
THE FINAL BLOW	63
NO ESCAPING IT	65

PART FOUR—I've Got To Change! **67**

GOD PLEASE HELP ME!	67
TIME TO LIVE IT	68
WHAT HAPPENED TO MATT?	70
THE MORE YOU GIVE, THE MORE YOU RECEIVE	71
SPONSOR SOMEONE	72
TRYING TO CHANGE	75
TIME TO CONFESS	77
LENT	80
EASTER	83
NOW WHAT CAN I DO FOR GOD?	83
JESUS, IF THAT'S YOU, PROVE IT	84
SATURDAY NIGHT PRAYER GROUP	88
MAJOR DISAPPOINTMENT	91
BACKSLIDING	92
IS IT ALL WORTH IT?	95
BE A SAINT	97
A YEAR GONE BY	98
THE ATTACK	99
TESTIMONY	101
RETREAT	102
WEEKLY PRAYER GROUP MEETINGS	104

WHICH PATH WILL YOU FOLLOW?	105
BLAST FROM THE PAST	106
THE WAY TO ME	109
CONCLUSION	**113**
EPILOGUE—About this book and others I have written	**126**

This picture was taken of me in Canada on a fishing trip just one week before I experienced what you are about to read.

PART ONE—I Never Thought This Would Happen to Me

METAL THUNDER

Brent and I slipped quietly through the basement door of his parent's house around midnight and tiptoed out to his car. We popped it into neutral and pushed it down their paved driveway, hoping his parents wouldn't hear us. After reaching a safe distance from the house, I fired up the engine, and we headed back to the party we had left just an hour before.

It was the second week of summer after our junior year of high school. It was also Brent's seventeenth birthday. He wanted to get drunk, so I offered to be his designated driver. I figured it was the best gift I could give him since I didn't have any money to buy him a present. Brent was one of the more popular kids in my class, so I was trying extra hard to get him to like me. My hope was that he would invite me to hang out with him and his friends more often.

Being Brent's designated driver turned out to be a difficult gift for me to give because the annoying drunks at the party were driving me crazy! They were slurring and slobbering all over the place and acting like complete idiots. The girl I liked was upstairs doing who knows what with some guy, which added to my misery. As I sat by myself on the couch, I noticed a large brown bowl of pretzels on the coffee table. I thought I could find a little consolation in eating them, but that didn't work because they were disgustingly stale and mushy.

There was a glimmer of hope that Brent and I would have to leave when Todd arrived and announced that cops were heavily patrolling the area. This concerned me because we were way out in the country. A cop car in that area was extremely rare and almost unheard of. "We'd better get out of here," I frantically thought. I suggested to Brent that we get in the car and go back to his house. Unfortunately, he didn't want to leave because he was trying to hook up with some girl. I recommended that we at least move the car to Todd's house in case we needed to make a run for it.

Todd overheard our conversation and asked, "Are you talking about moving the car to my house?"

ME: Yeah, is that okay?

(*I figured he wouldn't mind since his parents went away every weekend, and no one was ever home at his house.*)

TODD: Sure, let me give you a ride back.

ME: No thanks. It's only a two-minute walk.

(*He strongly insisted.*)

TODD: Let me give you a ride back!

(*I didn't like the idea, so I asked,*)

ME: Are you okay to drive?

TODD: Yeah, I'm fine!

(*In a very drawn out way, I repeated my questions with a strong tone of reluctance.*)

ME: Are you SURE you're okay to drive?

(*He confidently and boldly responded,*)

TODD: Dude! I'm totally fine!

Since I didn't want him to keep pestering me in front of everyone, I reluctantly accepted his offer. In an attempt to justify my decision, I told myself that he was probably okay to drive since he had just arrived at the party and I hadn't seen him drink anything. I was still a little concerned because Todd had a reputation for drinking and driving on a regular basis.

We went outside and got in the cars. I drove Brent's car up the street. Todd and his friend followed close behind in Todd's Mustang GT. When we got to Todd's house, I parked Brent's car and we both got out. Brent climbed into the back seat of the Mustang first, and I followed close behind.

The Mustang only had room for two passengers in the back seat. It was very uncomfortable because we both had to squeeze tightly into one seat. I looked over at the other seat to see why we were so cramped. To my surprise, there was a case of beer sitting there. This concerned me, but I didn't make an issue of it since we would be out of the car in less than forty seconds. All he had to do was drive back down the road, pull into the driveway, and turn the car off. As we pulled out of his driveway, I jokingly said, "Hey Todd, light um up!" I thought it would be neat to do a little burnout in a Mustang. He didn't do it, so I thought to myself, "Ahh no big deal." My thoughts went back to the party and how dreadful it was for me there.

Todd drove down the road toward the party but didn't pull into the driveway. Instead, he pulled onto the road next to the house where the party was and brought the car to a complete stop. It was a straight road often used for midnight drag racing. I didn't realize what he was doing until he punched the gas. Smoke filled the air along with the high-pitched sound of squealing tires. I slammed on my seatbelt with lightning speed. My body filled with panic, and I tightly held my breath! My fingers sank deeply into the seat as I gripped it with all my might. The highest number on the speedometer was 85. Within seconds the needle disappeared out of sight. I estimate we were going at least 100 miles per hour. We sped down the road at a frightening rate of speed until he finally let off the gas and slowly brought the car to a stop. He then turned the car around. Facing the direction we had just come from, he nailed the gas and peeled out for a second time. The needle quickly disappeared beyond 85 again.

At the end of the road was a "T" shaped intersection. Our only options were to go left or right, NOT STRAIGHT! We approached the intersection at an alarming rate of speed. I looked at the stop sign, then to the speedometer, then back to the stop sign. The engine raced! My heart pounded! My anxious thoughts were, "Okay. He knows his car. He knows how long it takes to stop. We are going to stop. We're going to be fine."

I had been in many situations where I didn't think the driver would stop their car in time, but they always managed to do so. We were dangerously close to the intersection when he finally locked up the brakes. The tires screamed! In my little world, everything seemed to become dead silent, and we started to move in slow motion. The speedometer came creeping back from the grave as it slowly lowered beneath the 85 mile per hour mark. The last thing I remember *thinking* as the car began to slide slightly to the right side was, "We're going to make it. We'll slide right around the turn and be fine." The last thing I remember *seeing* was the stop sign flash past my head. At that moment a loud roar of metal thunder ripped through the still night. We had smashed head-on into a tree at about 75 miles per hour. Just writing about it gives me the chills to this day.

If you don't deal well with blood and trauma, I suggest you skip the rest of Part One and go straight to Part Two of this book!

It must have been at least thirty minutes before I regained consciousness. I was slumped over like a dead man. The first thing I did as my eyes began to open was slowly sit up. My lower lip had been severed from the center to the right side. It was dangling by a little piece of skin at the far right-hand corner of my mouth. As I reached an upright sitting position, my lip bounced against my chin. I frantically thought, "Oh no, MY LIP! I am going to be ugly for the rest of my life! I am never going to have a girlfriend again!"

I didn't know how badly I was hurt, or if I was going to survive. All I knew was that I was completely covered in blood. My white shirt was now deep dark red. My arms were heavily caked with thick, dark, coagulated blood. This prompted me to say a prayer to prepare myself for death. Without hesitation, I recited the "Hail Mary," a prayer I had learned as a little child.

After I had finished my prayer, I continued to wonder how bad my condition was. I thought that maybe one or two of my front teeth were knocked out, but I didn't dare check. The braces I had worn for three and a half *painfully long* years had been taken off just two months before. I didn't want to know for sure how many teeth, if any, were knocked out. The metal wire retainer that was clamped to my lower molars and went *behind* my bottom teeth was now in *front* of my lower teeth, which was extremely uncomfortable and annoying.

At this point, I went into denial thinking, "This isn't happening to me! This doesn't happen to me! This kind of thing happens to someone else, not me! I am supposed to grow up, fully enjoy my life, and die at an old age. I am NOT supposed to have any problems! I am supposed to be happy and healthy and fulfill all of my dreams." I hoped I would wake up at any moment from this bad dream, but that never happened. This was real!

This picture was taken of the car a few days after the accident. I sat behind the seat you can see. My knees bent the seat in the middle and my face hit the top left side, twisting it forward.

The next thing I remember was a paramedic vigorously shaking my right leg. When I opened my eyes, he started screaming, "WAIT A MINUTE, WAIT A MINUTE, HE IS ALIVE! HE IS ALIVE!" There were people yelling and screaming all around the car. The paramedic asked me my name, age, address, and phone number. While my mind was hurting and concentrating as hard as it could trying to remember the information, my mouth was just saying it. It seemed as if I wasn't the one saying the words because they were coming out of my mouth before I could even think of them. After I gave the information, he asked a woman paramedic to go call my parents. I then had a chance to ask him the question I was most concerned about, "Am I going to live?" He asked, "Do you want the truth?" "Yes," I said. He paused and looked down for a moment with a somewhat sad look on his face. He then looked back up at me and hesitantly said, "I don't know. You look really bad." This was a bit difficult for me to hear. I thought that paramedics were supposed to be positive and give you hope. I sat there motionless, pondering death. "Is this my time? Is my life actually about to end? I'm so young! Will anyone even care if I die? Will anyone come to my funeral?" I felt so unprepared for death. Eventually my thoughts began to shift. I was trying to hang on. I then forcefully thought to myself, "NO! I'M NOT GOING TO DIE! I AM GOING TO LIVE!"

While this was going on in my head, the paramedic asked me if I had been drinking alcohol. I had hit my head so hard that I was having trouble remembering anything. I answered,

ME: I don't know.

(*He responded in a severe tone.*)

PARAMEDIC: I need to know! It is very important! Now tell me! Were you drinking or not?

(*I tried as hard as I could to remember but couldn't. As I looked at the situation, I thought that maybe I had started drinking since I was in the back seat instead of the driver's seat.*)

ME: I don't know. I know I wasn't drinking at first, but I can't remember now.

(*He sounded even more intense each time he asked me.*)

PARAMEDIC: I NEED TO KNOW! WERE YOU DRINKING OR NOT?

I was frustrated because I couldn't remember. His questioning really annoyed me and made the situation ten times more difficult. I was suffering from a serious concussion. All I wanted to do was sleep. At this point, the woman paramedic came back and said, "We keep getting an answering machine at his parent's house." He yelled, "Then send the police to his house, NOW!" I anxiously thought, "Oh no! I am in serious trouble now! My parents are going to kill me! There is no way I'm getting out of this one!"

Despite my nervousness, I kept passing out. The paramedic yelled, "Make sure you stay awake! We don't want you falling asleep and slipping into a coma!" This really concerned me, and I thought, "Oh no, a coma!" It was very difficult to remain awake. No matter how hard I tried I just couldn't do it. Every time I opened my eyes I fought to keep them open, worried that I might not get another chance. Then the paramedic said, "Hold on, we can't get you out of the car until last."

The passengers in the front seat were taken away in the first two ambulances that arrived on the scene while I remained trapped in the back. The next thing I remember was opening my eyes to see the paramedic hovering over me with a blanket. He explained that he was protecting me from flying chunks of glass and metal as they cut off the roof of the car in order to get me out. Thoughts ripped through my mind. "WHAT? ME! THEY ARE USING THE JAWS OF LIFE FOR ME?" I always thought the Jaws of Life were used to cut the roof off cars that had been in serious accidents, and the people inside were often dead. This did not encourage me at all.

The roof came off, and five people jumped into the car. They all put their arms around me and prepared to lift. The lead paramedic's face was inches from mine. He yelled out, "Okay everybody, on three! One! Two!" As he called out the number two, my body shifted and my head rolled from the upright position down to the side. He screamed, "WAIT! WAIT! DON'T LIFT HIM! HIS NECK MIGHT BE BROKEN! HIS NECK MIGHT BE BROKEN!" "Oh great," I discouragingly thought to myself, "My neck might be broken too!" I didn't want to even think about the possibility of being paralyzed! They quickly fastened a neck brace around my neck and lifted me out of the car. I vividly remember them laying me on a stiff board before lifting me onto the stretcher. It was a hot June night. The board felt shockingly cold because it had been in the air-conditioned ambulance. It made me gasp in a breath of air when my blood soaked T-shirt came in contact with it.

They strapped me onto the stretcher and laid a heavy metal tank between my legs. With this in place and the big brace around my neck, I was powerless. The only parts of my body I could move were my eyelids. Almost as soon as I was in the ambulance I lost consciousness. I woke up only twice during the ride. The first time was when we came to a screeching stop. I could feel the weight of my body being drawn forward as the driver hit the brakes hard. Before I opened my eyes, I envisioned paramedics with panic-stricken faces hovering over me yelling out commands; fighting to keep me alive. I also thought I would see IV bottles swinging all around from the turbulent ambulance ride. When my eyes finally opened, I was upset to see that no one was even there. There were no people, no tubes, no IV bottles, and no frantic yelling. There was nothing. I thought to myself, "Am I that bad that they are not even going to try to save me? Don't they even care?" The situation really bothered me, but within seconds I went unconscious again. The second time I woke I hoped to find at least one person watching over me, but there were none.

AT THE HOSPITAL

We arrived at the hospital. I imagined they would rush me down the hallway and into an emergency room for surgery in an attempt to save my life. What actually happened was a bit different. They took me out of the ambulance, into the hallway, and then they just walked away. As I lay there alone in the hallway, I frantically thought, "WHAT IS GOING ON? DON'T THEY EVEN CARE THAT I MIGHT DIE HERE?"

Finally, a doctor came over to me. He picked up my lip, fondled it in his fingers right in front of my face and said, "Yeah, we *might* be able to save that." I thought with a frantic scream, "WHAT DO YOU MEAN **MIGHT** BE ABLE TO SAVE IT? THAT'S MY LIP, MAN!" Then he heartlessly and carelessly dropped my lip. It bounced lifelessly against my cheek and then hung down to the side of my face. This overwhelmingly upset me, and there was nothing I could do about it!

Before long I passed out again. I woke up when they started wheeling me into the intensive care unit. They put me in a bed and placed a heart rate monitor on my finger. The nurse just sat there intently looking at me. There was so much sorrow and compassion pouring out of her eyes. We were both helpless. I was physically disabled, and she was powerless because of the law. She said, "Legally, I am not allowed to touch you without parental consent since you are under the age of eighteen. All I can do is sit here and make sure you don't die."

NEAR DEATH EXPERIENCE?

It was silent in my hospital room except for the beeping noise coming from the heart rate monitor. Since there was nothing else to do, I laid there listening to the slow beep noise. Beep, beep, beep. After a while the beeping noise was suddenly replaced by an unbroken eerie sound "Beeeeeeeeeee." My eyes opened wide with panic as I listened to the monitor "flat line," which indicated that I no longer had a heartbeat. I waited for death to follow. I expected to see big lights from heaven break through the ceiling of the room as the moment of my death arrived. I waited, and waited, and waited, but death never came. In an attempt to understand the situation, I began to look around the room. Eventually I looked down at my hand and discovered that the heart rate monitoring device had slipped off my finger. The tension in my shoulders dropped in a sigh of relief when I made this discovery. If I wasn't going to die from the accident, I thought I might die from a heart attack caused by the heart rate monitor scaring me to death. This happened two more times. Each time, I went through the same cycle of thinking I was about to die before realizing that the monitoring device had slipped off my finger.

THE SITUATION I NEVER WANTED TO BE IN

Sometime later I woke to a mad rush of both male and female nurses running into the room. The head nurse called out, "We just got word from your parents!" In an instant, my clothes were cut away from my body. I lay there completely naked and powerless in front of total strangers. Throughout my life I had always dreaded the idea of being in that situation. The thought of being seen naked by total strangers completely embarrassed me. Now that it was actually happening, I was surprised that I just didn't care. I was helpless and there was nothing I could do about it.

They began to scrub off the blood to assess my condition. The nurse standing next to me said she was going to give me some stabilization shots as she prepared a *huge* metal needle. Being a seventeen year old *man*, I said with assertive courage, "Okay, give them to me!" In my mind I thought, "Yeah, go ahead. Right there in my arm. I can take it!" I mentally prepared myself to withstand the sharp sting it would cause when she plunged the large needle into my shoulder muscle. As soon as it was ready, she said, "Okay Sean, I'm going to need you to roll onto your side for me." I didn't know why she asked me to do that until I felt the needle suddenly spike me in the butt. This was an unexpected, embarrassing surprise, and I thought to myself, "WHAT? I can take it in the arm!" Then, disappointed, I thought, "So much for taking it like a man." They proceeded to shove three separate IVs into my arms, and put oxygen tubes into my nose. But the only thing I could think about was my lip. I kept wondering when they were going to fix it. It was three or four in the morning when the nurses finally informed me that the specialist who would perform my surgery was not available until nine the next morning. This had me very concerned because I didn't know if my dangling lip would last that long.

PROVIDING A SAMPLE

The next ordeal involved a urine sample. Providing one was never a problem for me before that night. Talk about bad timing! I think I was overly self-conscious about having to go to the bathroom while lying in a bed with strangers in the room. They kept telling me they were going to have to obtain a sample if I could not provide one. The procedure for extracting a sample sounded rather painful, and I did *not* want to experience it! I responded, "Just give me a few minutes! I'll give you a sample." The nurse was very understanding. She gave me some soda hoping it would help. She held a straw in the left-hand corner of my mouth where I still had some lip. While I drank, I was careful to *not* touch the front of my mouth with my tongue because I still did not want to know if any of my teeth had been knocked out.

As soon as the nurse walked out of the room, I felt a violent, strong nausea come over me. I desperately pushed the emergency call button with a relentless fervor. Before she came back, I vomited all over myself. They had to completely strip both the bed and me. To do this, they wheeled another bed into my room and lifted me onto it. After they put new sheets on my bed, they put a new hospital gown on me. When that whole ordeal was taken care of, I had to refocus on my problem of providing a urine sample. I was eventually able to provide one without their intrusive assistance. Thank God!

MY PARENTS

My parents arrived at the hospital. My dad was the first one in to see me. I remember looking up to see him enter the room. He slowly came in and walked around to the left-hand side of the bed.

He did not speak at first, but his eyes said it all. "My boy, my poor little boy, oh look at my son." Judging by the look on his face I don't know how he was able to keep from crying. Tears come to my eyes as I think back and write about it now. It saddens me to picture his face and the concern he was feeling for me. I remember him holding my hand and gently running his fingers through my hair like he did when I was a little boy. He used to do that to help me fall asleep at night. In the mean time, my mom entered the room and sat on my right side. I couldn't move much. I didn't know what to say, so I didn't say anything except, "Sorry."

THE PRIEST

A priest from the Catholic high school I attended was the next person in to see me. Almost immediately after he arrived, he gave me a Sacrament known as the "Anointing of the Sick." He did this by anointing my head with sacred oil and praying over me. I remembered learning in school that this Sacrament was once called "Last Rites" because it was given to people right before they died. The use and understanding of the Sacrament expanded over time. It is now also given to people who are sick and in need of healing. Even though I knew this, I found myself dwelling on the fact that it used to be called "Last Rites." I wondered if getting anointed meant I was expected to die soon. Before the priest left, we prayed some common prayers together know as the "Our Father," "Hail Mary," and "Glory Be." It was nice to have him there to pray with me, and I was sad to see him go.

SURGERY, IS IT GOING TO HURT?

The night passed. In the morning, the nurses prepared me for surgery. I had never broken a bone or had surgery before. I was nervously wondering, "What is it going to be like? Am I going to be in a lot of pain? Will I be able to feel the doctor operating? Will I remember anything?" My time finally arrived. They wheeled me into the surgery room. I think they gave me some final shots, and then the surgeon placed a large red gas mask over my nose. He asked me some questions, then had me count backwards from nine. I frantically thought to myself, "NINE! There is

12   I've Got To Change

NO WAY I am going to be unconscious by the time I reach zero!" Even though I was afraid, I slowly began counting, "Nine, eight, sevvvvv," and I was out.

DOCTORS REPORT

After I woke up from the surgery, the doctors came and gave me a report on my overall condition. My lower jaw had broken completely in half in the front and in two places on the left side. To correct the break in the front, they made an incision behind my chin, pulled the flesh up out of the way, screwed a metal plate into my lower jaw to hold it together, and then stitched my skin back together. They couldn't do anything surgically for the two breaks on the left side of my jaw, so they put me on a liquid diet for two months. This was done so that I would not aggravate the breaks by chewing while they healed. The doctors went on to say that one of my bottom front teeth was knocked out and two were severely loosened. The two that were loosened were wired to my retainer to hold them in place. The doctors hoped the roots of those two teeth would retake, so that I could keep them.

Probably the hardest thing for me to hear was that *six* of my upper front teeth were knocked out, and my upper jaw was shattered and gone. They had packed my upper jaw with freeze-dried bone in order to rebuild it, and then stitched my gums back together with nearly a hundred dissolvable stitches. As you already know, half of my lower lip had been cut off. I was relieved that they were able to sew it back on. They expected my lip to look fairly normal once the stitches were removed, but they explained that the nerves in my lip may never fully recover. Next, they told me that a piece of glass had gone completely through the upper portion of my right ear. They easily repaired it with a single stitch. They said that my right collarbone broke in half and punctured ten percent of my right lung. This caused internal bleeding and breathing problems which is why I still had oxygen tubes in my nose. This frightened me a little. Lastly, they found blood in my urine sample. They said this was a bad sign. It could mean kidney failure. The seatbelt I was wearing during the car accident did more damage than good because it did not have a shoulder strap.

It surprised me that I had so much wrong with me. Before I heard their report, I thought my only real problem was my dangling lip.

SIDE EFFECTS

A second priest from my high school came to visit me later that afternoon. He also gave me the Sacrament of the Anointing of the Sick. "I must be in real bad shape to be anointed again!" I thought to myself. We prayed together, and then he left.

Soon after the priest left, I had to go for testing on my kidneys. The procedure required me to sign a consent form. They wanted to inject me with a dye in order to x-ray my kidneys. The nurse recited a list of possible side effects from the dye, one of which was death. A thought screamed loudly through my mind, "DEATH! AND YOU WANT ME TO SIGN FOR THIS?" I didn't like the idea but felt I had no choice but to sign. Since I couldn't move my right arm, the nurse told me to try signing with my left hand. I tried to keep a sense of humor about everything and jokingly remarked that my left-handed signature looked like "chicken scratch." The nurses all laughed, and then wheeled me in for the x-rays. Later, the doctors came to my room to tell me that there was no threatening damage to my kidneys. I was relieved to hear that!

FORMER BEST FRIEND

My last visitor in the intensive care unit was my old best friend, Eli. He and I were the same age. He lived at the other end of my road and went to the local public school. I would have done anything for him. He was like a brother to me. I was closer to him than I was to my own family. I always put him before anyone else, including whatever girl I was dating at the time.

The best example of this occurred when we were freshmen in high school. I had recently started going out with one of the prettiest girls in my school. We made plans to go to a movie. It was my first official date as a high school student. Eli called me about a half hour before my parents were going to take me to the movie. He asked me what I was doing. Excitedly, I told him, "I am about to leave for my first date with Liz!" In a sad tone of voice he said,

"Oh." Still filled with excitement I asked, "What are you doing tonight?" In a depressed tone of voice he said, "Nothing. I'll probably just sit around and watch TV." I felt so bad for him. I didn't want him to have to stay home alone, so I invited him to come with us. He immediately cheered up and joyfully accepted my invitation. I quickly called Liz to make sure she was okay with the idea. She agreed, so the three of us went to the movies. I did my best to show them an equal amount of attention the whole night so that neither of them felt neglected.

I referred to Eli as my *old* best friend because by the middle of our junior year of high school he got his first steady girlfriend and dropped me like a ton of bricks. It killed me when he did that. I felt as if I had gone through a divorce or something. Because of his decision to end our friendship, we hadn't seen or spoken to each other in several months. In fact, the whole reason I was hanging out with Brent the night of the car accident was because I was actively looking for a new group of friends since Eli and I no longer spoke to each other.

I had never expected to see Eli again. The only thing I could think when he walked into my hospital room was, "He... he's here. He still cares." He came in and sat by my bedside. I was really glad to see him. He told me he was sorry for what he had done. He also promised we would hang out again when I got out of the hospital. I really appreciated him saying that, but was disappointed later when he didn't deliver on his promise.

WHAT HAPPENED TO THE OTHER GUYS IN THE CAR?

Of all the passengers in the vehicle the night of the accident, I was the only one sober. The driver lied to me; he was drunk. He had been drinking before he even got to the party. I was the only one wearing a seat belt, yet my injuries seemed worse than those of the other three passengers combined. Brent had miraculously rolled between the two front seats during the accident which left him almost untouched. He ended up with cuts on his right arm and leg from elbowing out the sunroof and climbing out of the car. He went into the house where the party was, and took a shower. It hurt me when I learned that. I felt like he just left me there to die. The driver broke his collarbone, needed stitches in his chin, and sprained his ankle. The passenger in front of me broke his right arm, needed some stitches, and had a severe concussion.

STOLEN HEART

After almost a week in the hospital, I got out of bed and made my way to the bathroom for the first time. The nurses wheeled my IVs behind me. I felt as if my heart was taken from me the moment I entered the bathroom and looked in the mirror. My face was so swollen that it looked like a pumpkin on my shoulders! I had no idea I looked like that. The thought never crossed my mind. I had assumed I looked normal except for the stitches in my lip and the bandage on my chin. "People have actually been seeing me like this?" I sadly thought to myself. Seeing myself in the mirror seriously hurt my feelings. It inaugurated an intense mental and emotional suffering to join with my physical pain.

DON'T YOU WANT TO BEAT HIM UP?

One of the nuns from my Church came to visit me. She anointed my head with oil. This made me wonder if my condition was worse than they were telling me. I also wondered how many times I was going to be anointed.

During that same week, many people asked me if I wanted to beat up the driver for doing this to me. My response was always a quick, "No." My focus was on recovering, not complaining or seeking vengeance. I knew that nothing I said or did could change what had happened. I dealt with the situation by accepting it and moving on with my life. I also knew that it wasn't entirely the driver's fault. I was the one who snuck out of the house with Brent and went to the party. I was the one who got into Todd's car that night. I knew it was wrong to be involved with underage drinking, but I did it anyway. I faced the overall reality of my situation and **took total responsibility for my actions**.

Do you have any actions or decisions that you still need to take total responsibility for in your own life?

GOD'S GRACE

Years later, I realized that I was only able to view my situation as maturely as I had because God had granted me many graces through the Sacrament of the Anointing of the Sick and through the prayers of my family and Church. This didn't occur to me at first because I didn't *feel* anything happen when I received the Sacrament. At that age, I didn't realize that faith and feelings are *not* the same thing, and that we should not base our faith exclusively on feelings.

Because of God's grace, it seemed easy to forgive the driver and not be resentful. I was able to be realistic and take responsibility for my actions. What seemed like normal, obvious behavior to me seemed utterly absurd to many of the people I knew. God's grace was the only explanation.

WHEN CAN I GO HOME?

After my surgery, there wasn't much more the hospital could do for me. The only thing left for me to do was endure the slow lengthy healing process. They let me go home as soon as I could breathe well enough without the oxygen tubes and consume enough nutrition on my own without depending on the IVs.

This picture of me was taken just a few days before I was sent home from the Hospital. It wasn't even three weeks after the picture of me in Canada at the beginning of the book. Think of how much your life can change in an incredibly short period of time!

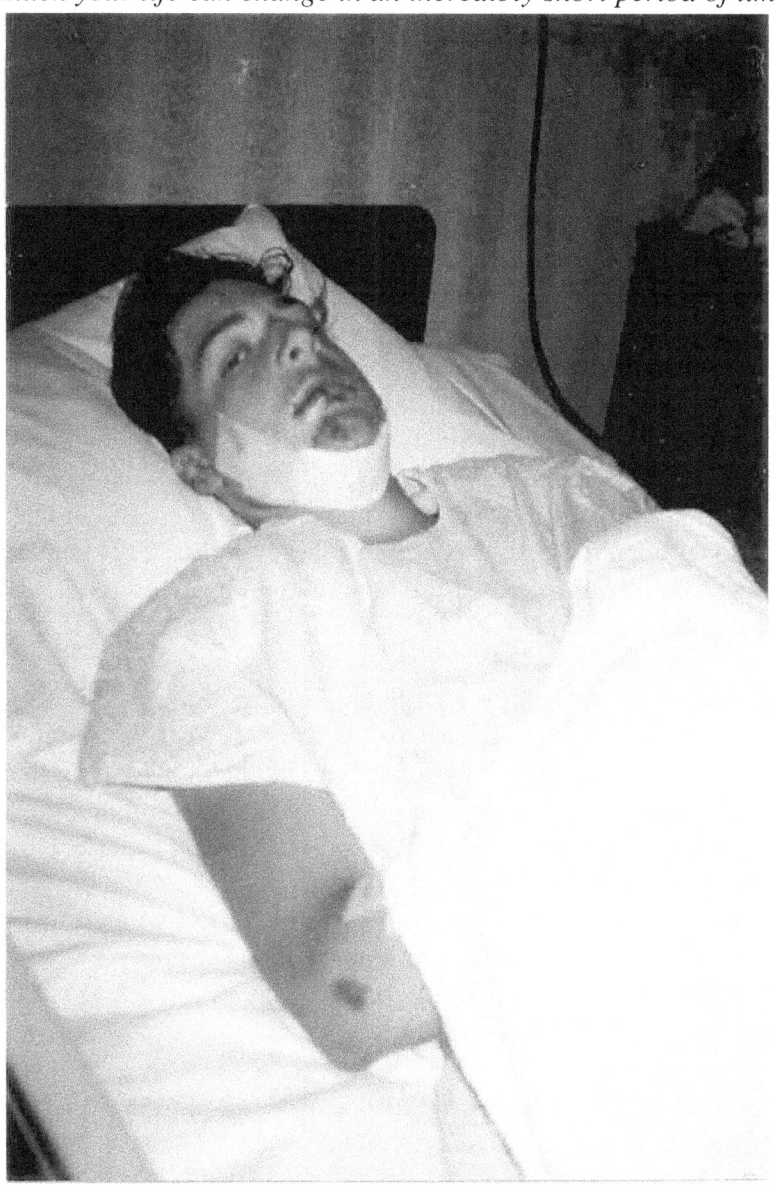

PART TWO—Out of the Hospital and Senior Year

IF I WOULD HAVE DIED

Just two weeks after the accident, I was back at home. I had difficulty breathing and tired out very easily because of my punctured lung. This, along with my other injuries, left me fairly inactive throughout the summer. My condition forced me to do a lot of sitting, which in turn caused me to do a lot of thinking. The most prominent question I asked myself was, "If I would have died, would I have gone to heaven?" I forced myself to be perfectly honest. The true answer was very obvious to me. The answer was "No!" I knew I was not fit for heaven because of certain choices I had made in my life. Death always seemed far off in the distance before the car accident. I figured I could get away with doing things I knew were wrong because I planned to straighten out later on in life. I thought I would get to do all the things I ever wanted to do without any problems. I thought I would grow up, go off to college, get married, have a family, have a good job, and live to be about eighty.

The reality is that any of us, including myself, could die today! It could be an hour from now. It could be in five minutes. We just never know when it will happen. Not acknowledging that we are going to die, and not facing the fact that it could be at any moment, does not help us prepare for it. After facing the reality of my own death, and how close it could be, I resolved to be the best person I could be at every moment of every day. I wanted to be ready for my death and judgment before God. I strongly believed that I needed to choose to follow God's ways in order to go to heaven. No longer was I going to take chances by doing things I knew were wrong.

From these thoughts, I developed a plan to improve. My plan started with a self evaluation at the end of each day. I would do this by asking myself, "If I would have died today, would I have gone to heaven?" If my answer was "No," I would immediately know why. The things that would keep me out of heaven dramatically stood out in my mind. I would then make amends by choosing to *change* those areas of my life, so that I could answer "Yes" to my question at the end of the next day.

When I started these daily examinations, the aspect of my life that I felt the worst about was my abuse of alcohol on a few occasions. With my new outlook, I resolved not to drink again until I was at the legal drinking age. I also needed to come to terms with the fact that peer pressure, and being made fun of for my virginity, had influenced me to think that it was okay to have sex before marriage. This was in direct opposition to what I was taught in Catholic school. The Catholic Church teaches that premarital sex is wrong in God's eyes. As a result, I renewed my commitment to save myself for marriage in order to follow God's ways. It was difficult going against what everyone else was saying, but I knew it was far better than going to hell because I allowed peer pressure and secular views separate me from God. I also made a conscious effort to stop using so much foul language.

When I was very young, I viewed foul language as something extremely bad because my mom would wash my mouth out with liquid soap when she heard me say a bad word. When I was in seventh grade, it became more important for me to be liked by my classmates than to worry about whether or not foul language was wrong. Because of this, and because I knew my mom wasn't there to wash my mouth out with soap, I started quoting a very foul-mouthed comedian when I was around my classmates in order to make them laugh. Over the years, my use of foul language had become much more habitual. After the car accident, I wanted to stop using it.

Lastly, I had to address my cheating problem in school. I had struggled with school my whole life. I even had to repeat third grade because my grades were barely passing. After repeating third grade, and still not doing much better, I began to develop methods of cheating in order to make decent grades. By the time I was in high school, I realized that my classmates were way ahead of me. They had learned the material while I had not. It really showed when the teachers asked questions that built on material we should have learned in previous years. Wanting to be the best person I could be, and realizing how much cheating had hurt me in life, I resolved never to cheat again. The grades that I would earn would be from my own honest efforts.

Although much of my time was spent thinking about the past and present, and how I could improve as a person, there was one other concept that seemed to haunt my mind. This one thought was different from all the others because it concerned the future. The fact that I survived the car accident made me believe that there was something really big and important I was supposed to do with my life some day. I just didn't know what it was.

THIS CAME AS A SURPRISE

Much to my surprise, I went on a few dates that summer. I never expected that to happen because I didn't have any teeth, had stitches all over my lip and chin, and my face was seriously swollen. I looked awful. The girl that dated me was the girl who had the party the night of the car accident. She started coming over to my house to visit me several times a week after I got home from the hospital. I didn't realize that I was going to be tested right away on several of my new convictions.

After I healed enough, she started taking me to parties. She would drink, but I refused. Two weeks later she came on to me very strongly and asked me to have sex with her. I couldn't believe what was happening. Despite the temptation, it remained clear to me that I must do what was right so that I would be ready for heaven if I died that day. Without any hesitation, I said, "No," then distanced myself from her. We stopped spending time together within a few weeks. I then reflected back on all that had happened. I was very proud of myself for the choices I made concerning alcohol and sex. It surprised me that she had even asked me to have sex with her. Nothing like that had ever happened to me before.

The testing did not stop there. An old girlfriend, Joan, invited me over to her house. She was the first girl I had ever kissed. It turned out that her parents were away for the weekend, and her best friend Tara was spending the night.

I felt uncomfortable because I was very self-conscious about my looks after the accident. Not having teeth was embarrassing, and it was very difficult for me to talk normally. Before I lost all my front teeth, I never realized how many sounds in our speech involve using our tongue against our teeth. The hardest pronunciations for me to make were TH, T and D.

Motivated by my poor self-image, I said out loud, "I'm ugly." In response, Tara said, "I think you're still hot!" She then sexually propositioned me. I didn't respond to her, but diverted their attention to the movie that was playing on the television.

The next thing I knew one of them brought out some alcohol and offered it to me. I declined. Tara then made it very obvious that she wanted me to get in bed with the two of them. Joan seemed a little uncomfortable with her suggestion, but didn't say anything.

I couldn't believe what was happening. This was the kind of situation I used to wish would happen to me before I renewed my convictions and realized the importance of living a life ready for death and judgment. Sleeping with these girls would have given me so much ammunition to brag about to the other guys in my class. All the people who teased me about my virginity would be silenced if I told them about this. Although it was not easy, I chose to do what was right and eventually went home.

After that, I thought to myself, "What is going on? What is prompting girls to proposition me all of a sudden? Is there a sign on my back that says, 'If you want a challenge, try getting me to have sex with you?' Why are girls trying to get me in bed now that I have firmly decided to save sex for marriage?"

22 I've Got To Change

This picture was taken within a few weeks after I came home from the hospital. If you look closely, you can see some of the white dissolvable stitches still remaining in my upper jaw. You can also see the metal wire around my two bottom teeth in the front, which held them in place. Lastly, you can see the collarbone brace. It was very humiliating for me to have this picture taken. It also emotionally hurt me to hear people laugh at me when they saw this picture.

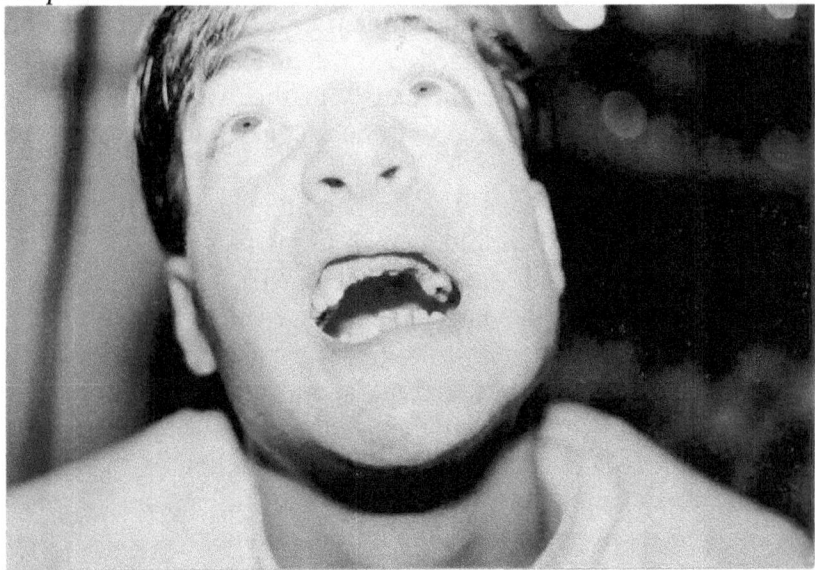

CRUSHED

It took almost two months for my upper jaw to heal enough to support dentures. Virtually all of the swelling in my face was gone, but I was deeply disturbed that my face was still bigger than it was supposed to be. The doctor hadn't realigned my jaw correctly, which caused it to stick out and up on my left side. I had always liked the way I looked before. Now I *hated* the way I looked! It was like looking at a total stranger every day in the mirror. I wanted to have surgery to fix it, but the doctor wouldn't do it. He told me to just chew on the other side of my mouth. He said that would build up the muscles on that side and make my face look more even. This deeply disturbed me. It was easy for him to say that because he wasn't in my position. My low self-esteem became even lower.

With a little more than a week left of summer, I was finally fitted with a denture plate. It gave me some relief to have teeth, but I was still embarrassed that I was seventeen years old and had to wear dentures. The night after I got my dentures, I decided to go with Brent to hang out on a street corner with some of our classmates. It would be my first night out with them all summer.

There were about fifteen people on the corner when we arrived. Some of the girls that were there had always intimidated me. Their attitude toward others simply frightened me. I didn't think there was anything I could do to get them to like me.

The killer blow happened the moment we walked up to the corner and Brent yelled, "Hey everybody, check this out. Yo, McVeigh, take your teeth out! Come on and show them your teeth, ha, ha, ha! It's so funny!" I was humiliated and *crushed*! I tried to hide my embarrassment, but there was one girl who seemed to notice how much the whole situation hurt me. While everyone else was laughing, she looked at me with understanding in her eyes and didn't laugh. I never would have expected that from her, since she intimidated me more than the other girls. As for the rest of them, they apparently had no idea how sensitive and self-conscious I was about my appearance and my false teeth.

The situation made me want to crawl under a rock and die. I ended up spending the next few hours of my life silently standing off to the side in the shadows feeling awful.

FIRST DAY BACK

The first day of my senior year of high school arrived. This was the year I had been waiting for since I took my first step into that high school. This was supposed to be the best year of my life. It was supposed to be the year I was on top of it all. Everyone was supposed to look up to the seniors. It was supposed to be easy to be liked by everyone because you were older and you "knew the ropes."

The start of my big year was nothing like I had dreamed it would be. The first day of school was horrible. Most of the returning students had heard about my car accident but hadn't seen me yet. I remember walking down the hall and getting stared at by nearly everyone. They wanted to see what I looked like, but no one talked to me. They tried to stare at me without getting caught, but I saw them all. It made me feel like an alien. It only got worse as the day progressed.

At lunchtime, I bought some food and sat down with the other seniors. I silently began to eat my food without even looking up at anyone. From across the table, an inconsiderate classmate of mine called out, "Hey McVeigh, don't take your dentures out man! I don't want to get grossed out while I'm trying to eat! Ha, ha, ha, ha, ha, ha!" He leaned back in his chair laughing along with many of the other students at the table. His comment ripped right through me like a steel dagger. He had humiliated me in front of everyone! Although his comment hurt me deeply, I simply said, "Thanks." In my mind I was thinking, "Do you want my heart with that too?"

I finished my day with thoughts of never going back to that school again. I didn't want to feel alienated and get ridiculed every day. If I went to a different school, no one would even know what had happened to me. Later in the evening, I was sitting in my bedroom trying to decide if I should leave my school. It was the only Catholic high school around, so I would have to go to public school if I left. Before long, I began to feel a very commanding courage coming from within me. With intense power, I spoke out loud, "No! I will not let them drive me away from school. I am not going to let them beat me down. I'm going back!"

I made a choice to focus on my own personal goals of growth, and not on the negative things some of my classmates had to say. This turned out to be extremely beneficial for my life. If you have difficulties with others the way I did, I recommend focusing on your own goals and ignoring their negativity.

NEXT TABLE OVER

I went back to that school, but I never went back to that lunch table. I sat at the next table over. After a while, there were three other senior guys who sat with me. We were a diverse bunch. One kid was a very popular basketball star. One was overweight, but everyone liked him because he was very funny and looked like a famous heavyset actor. The third guy was quiet around large groups of people, but he could definitely do his share of talking at our table.

ONE MORE TRIAL

I had to face one more difficult situation early in the year concerning my dentures. The seniors always did something "goofy" for their ID card pictures. Many of my senior classmates wanted me to take my dentures out for my picture because they thought it would be funny. They didn't seem to understand how terribly embarrassing that would be for me or how much it would hurt my feelings to hear them laugh at me every time they looked at my picture. I quietly declined every person that asked me to do this, but some people kept relentlessly pressuring me. They made me feel guilty for not doing what they wanted me to do. Despite their pressure, I held my ground and refused.

Being hurt by my classmates' inconsiderate jokes about my dentures enabled me to see the pain I had unknowingly caused other people by my sarcasm over the years. I used to make jokes about others to make my friends laugh. It wasn't until I was hurt by people's jokes about my dentures that I realized that no one likes to be made fun of. This experience taught me to treat others the way I wanted to be treated. I stopped making jokes about people, and found myself getting angry when I heard my classmates making fun of someone else. There was one student in particular that I felt bad for. Prior to my senior year, I had listened to my classmates jokingly ridicule him every day. Many times I joined in with them. It was easy to do, and it helped me fit in and be liked by my classmates. After my experience with the ID card picture, I vowed to change my ways. I stopped ridiculing others. I also spoke up when I heard my classmates making fun of someone else and wished someone would stand up for me when I was being made fun of.

What do you do in those types of situations? Do you make fun of people? Do you stand up for people who are being made fun of?

APPLY YOURSELF

Although school had been a major struggle for me all my life, I was prepared to give it my best effort in senior year. My goal was to make the honor roll on my own without cheating. I had never been able to do that before. While many of my classmates slacked off in senior year, I pressed on harder. It took me much longer than my classmates to do each assignment because I was such a slow reader, but I made myself put in the time. I also didn't play any sports that year because I needed time to heal. This made it possible for me to devote myself to the extra time I needed to study.

My senior year was a refining year for me. It seemed like I was overcoming my worst areas. I even went to daily Mass before lunch during Lent in an effort to be the best person I could be. Actively working to become a better person, and tangibly seeing all the positive changes in my life, made me think I would just keep getting better and better for the rest of my life! I began to believe I had the potential to become an extraordinarily good person. With every test and every assignment, I tried harder. As a result of my efforts, I made the honor roll for the first three marking periods. I felt I was truly becoming the person God intended me to be.

GIRLFRIEND

Approximately three months before senior year ended, I was at a bowling alley with some friends. We were shooting pool. Two girls were playing pool a few tables over. I thought one of them was good looking, so I eventually went over to talk to them. My friends came over and joined me after they saw that the conversation was going well. I liked the girl named Deb. Her friend Nancy started showing an interest in me, so I got her and my friend into a conversation. I then moved over to talk to Deb. Before long, it turned into a group discussion, and we all exchanged phone numbers.

Nancy called me two days later. We talked for a while and had a very nice conversation. The next day a surprise snow blizzard hit Pennsylvania. This left most people stranded indoors for three days. Since I was stuck at home, I ended up talking with Nancy on the phone for several hours each day. She seemed to say all the things I always wanted to hear. I started to really like her because of who I thought she was as an individual, rather than base my decision on her looks. This made me feel like I was being a good person.

The last serious girlfriend I had was way back in freshman year. I hadn't had a serious girlfriend since then because I spent all of my sophomore year trying to get one of my old girlfriends back. Every time it looked like we were going to get back together something happened to prevent it. Right before the school year ended she started going out with an upperclassman. It bothered me when she did that, but my year was *not wasted*! As I waited for her throughout the year, I closely watched all of my classmates who were in serious relationships. They all thought they were in love and were going to get married. I could clearly see that they were wrong, but there was something blinding their ability to see it for themselves. I ended up being right. Every one of those relationships broke up before we graduated from high school.

There was one other very important lesson I learned during my sophomore year while I was trying to get back together with my old girlfriend. I realized that the whole point of dating someone should be to see if that is the person you want to marry or not. You shouldn't just date someone for the sake of having fun.

Drawing from my observations and realizations, I concluded that there was no point in getting into any serious relationships at that time because marriage seemed like such a long way off. At most, I would go out on casual dates with girls here and there, but nothing very serious.

Now let me bring you back to the situation with Nancy. I was a high school senior on the brink of graduating. A lasting relationship that could lead to marriage seemed much more possible at the age of eighteen than it did at the age of fifteen. I felt I had everything figured out in life, and had a solid handle on how the world works. Plus, I had grown to really like this girl. I couldn't stop thinking about her, which is something I was not used to. I felt very mature about the situation, and thought that we had a lot of potential. After considering all of this information, I decided it was time for me to try a serious relationship to see if she was the

28 I've Got To Change

right girl for me to marry after college. I asked her to be my girlfriend, and she excitedly accepted.

WHAT ARE MY MORAL CONVICTIONS?

Several people played a significant role in the development of my convictions concerning appropriate sexual behavior in a dating relationship. This in turn had a major impact on how my relationship developed with my new girlfriend, Nancy.

Probably the most influential group was the guys at my lunch table. Every day throughout that entire school year they had told their sex stories and given vulgar details of what they did the weekend before and who they did it with. They tried relentlessly all year to talk me out of my resolve to save sex for marriage.

In addition to the lunch table gang, there were two very influential adults that impacted my moral convictions. They never asked me what my stance was on premarital sex. They just assumed I was running around trying to get girls in bed. Nearly every time they saw me going out with my friends, they made it a point to tell me to use protection when having sex.

These two groups of people had been influencing me throughout the year, but the newest influence regarding this topic was my girlfriend, Nancy. She knew I wanted to save sex for marriage. She accepted my decision, although she didn't see it as necessary. She felt strongly that we should at least allow ourselves to "fool around."

On the other end of the spectrum were the religion teachers I had throughout my years of Catholic school. They taught me the Catholic teachings on sexual morality. I knew the Catholic Church states that we are not supposed to have sex outside of marriage or engage in *any* sins of fornication. This means "*no fooling around.*" Simply put, you are not supposed to touch or rub someone else's "private areas" if you are not married to them. To do anything more than kiss was out of the question. There were even some people who thought open mouth kissing was wrong because it could easily lead into all the other things we are not supposed to do before marriage.

As you can see, the information I received from my Church's teachings was in direct opposition to the information I received from everyone else around me, including what was on TV. This caused me to become very conflicted over this issue. Seeing how much my classmates were *apparently* enjoying sex and fooling around, and not seeing any obvious negative repercussions for their behavior, caused me to question if those behaviors were actually wrong. Wouldn't God have done something if we were not supposed to be doing those things?

Over time I began to feel like I was missing out on something. As the situation evolved, I started resenting my Catholic faith for imposing a moral obligation of proper sexual behavior on me. It didn't happen overnight, but I eventually began to compromise between my Church's teachings and what the people around me were saying. I let myself believe that it was okay for me to "fool around," as long as I didn't "go all the way" and have sex.

The way I dealt with my guilty conscience was to compare myself to my classmates. I thought, "Well, I am not nearly as bad as they are. I don't fool around with just anyone like some guys do. Many of them are fooling around and having sex with as many girls as they possibly can. I'm not doing that. I am just fooling around with my girlfriend who I really care about." This made me feel like I was doing better than everyone else around me. Rather than compare myself to others, I should have judged myself according to the standard of right and wrong that I had been taught. Somewhere along the way I stopped asking myself the question, "If I would have died today, would I have gone to heaven?" If I had asked myself this question, I would have realized that "fooling around" was *not* okay for me to do.

FOOLPROOF PLAN

Nancy was having people over for a party because her parents were going away for the weekend. My friends at the lunch table found out about it and began pressuring me to have sex with her. They constantly said things like, "Don't even bother talking to us on Monday if you don't have sex stories to tell." I responded, "Well it looks like we won't be talking then because I am saving myself for marriage."

Before I got to Nancy's house the night of the party, I had developed a plan to ensure that we would *not* have sex. She told me when we first started going out that she would not let me near her if I ever drank alcohol around her because she once had a very abusive relationship with an alcoholic boyfriend. She had promised herself that she would never let that happen again.

My strategy the night of the party was to simply get drunk. I figured that by drinking, I wouldn't have to worry about the issue of sex because Nancy wouldn't come near me. At the same time, I knew that getting drunk and having sex were both wrong. I *rationalized* my decision by telling myself that sex outside of marriage seemed far worse than drinking.

During the party, Nancy and I played trivial pursuit with Deb and her new boyfriend. While we played, I drank a bottle of champagne. Nancy sat there and watched me do it. I was confident that my plan was foolproof, and there was nothing left for me to worry about. After the game ended, Nancy grabbed my hand and took me upstairs. She was literally all over me. I thought she would back off when I told her that I was drunk, but she didn't. Instead, she thanked me for being honest, and smothered me all the more. Weakened by alcohol and overcome by her advances, I ended up giving in. I gave away the most sacred gift I could ever offer someone and all I could think of was, "Well, at least now I can tell the guys."

I was ashamed of myself in the morning. To make matters even worse, I had a pounding headache. Sure the guys at the lunch table would reward me with their cheers, but that wasn't worth throwing away my virginity! THERE WAS NO BRINGING IT BACK! IT WAS GONE FOREVER! I wish I had thought about that before I went to Nancy's house that night. I urge you to consider this. Think before you act! THERE IS NO BRINGING YOUR VIRGINITY BACK! I wish I had realized back then that it is never a good idea to compromise ANY of your moral convictions or rationalize them away! Even though I had good intentions, I never should have let myself drink alcohol. It started me down the path of sin, which only got worse as time went on. Please don't make the same mistakes I made!

After I had fallen into this sexual sin, I asked God to forgive me in the quiet of my bedroom at home. At first I felt terrible and guilty for sinning. In an attempt to deal with my guilt, and salvage my mistake, I decided that I wanted Nancy to be the only person I ever slept with. I was prepared to work at our relationship with all my heart and marry her after we graduated from college.

It became easier for me to *rationalize* my sin away since I thought I was going to marry her. Thoughts went through my mind, "Well, I love her. I want to marry her. I want to stay with her. We already started. Nothing bad seemed to happen because of it, so why stop? The world doesn't seem any different because we had sex. Why did they always say it was so wrong? Why did they make sex outside of marriage seem like such a big bad sin?"

After about a month, I started to think our physical intimacy was a good thing because I found myself in love and happy! We even developed a plan for our future together. We would go off to college as we had planned before we started going out. After the first year, we would transfer to the same school and get married after graduating.

My life dream was to have a loving and supportive wife and a few happy children. My mom stayed home with my brother, sister, and me while we were growing up, and I wanted my children to have that same blessing. I wanted to be best friends with my wife. I wanted us to do everything together as a team. I imagined us working together to do all the yard work and housework. I wanted to have dual sinks in the master bathroom, so that we could brush our teeth standing side by side in the morning. I wanted us to take long walks in the evening and have matching bikes for when we wanted to go out for a ride. I wanted a middle class paying job in environmental or wildlife management. Lastly, I wanted an average sized house in the woods with a white wooden fence in the front yard.

Nancy's vision was much different than mine. All she cared about was becoming a lawyer and making a million dollars. She wanted to have a big mansion and hire people to do all the manual labor around the house, so that she would never have to lift a finger. This also included hiring someone to take care of our children while she was off developing her career. Her idea of marriage was difficult for me to deal with. She didn't have the team image I had. She seemed to care more about a career than family. It deeply bothered me that she didn't want to stay home with our kids like my mom did. Although we had very different ideas of marriage, I was willing to work it out.

Without even realizing it, I had acquired the same blindness that I had observed in all of my classmates who were engaging in premarital sex. I didn't realize that my sin was subtly pulling me away from God, and causing me to compromise my own hopes and dreams for married life. It caused me to doubt God and His commandments since nothing drastic seemed to happen to me for having sex with Nancy. This sin was like a slow infectious poison that polluted my soul without me even detecting it. *The fact that I was not dealing with my sin properly significantly added to the rapid spread of this deadly disease!*

DIDN'T SEE IT COMING

Much to my surprise and devastation, Nancy broke up with me out of the clear blue in the middle of the summer. It caught me so off guard. I didn't understand what happened. I thought we were in love. I begged her to change her mind but she wouldn't. She broke up with me because one of her old boyfriends was pursuing her, and she wanted to be available to date him. This destroyed me! I began to feel intensely physically ill while we were still on the phone. It felt like someone ripped my guts out, threw them on the ground, stomped on them, and then shoved them back into me. Deep emotional pain thrashed through my soul as tears drenched my face. No matter how hard I tried, I just couldn't stop crying! The *pain* I experienced that day was a new level of suffering for me. It was far worse than any pain I had ever experienced before. I am not exaggerating when I say that it *literally* and physically felt like I lost a part of me that day. As the pain devoured my soul, I began to think, "Never again am I going to do this! This hurts too much! I am not going to let this happen to me again!"

Late that night, Nancy called me and tried to get back together with me. She was crying and said she felt like she lost a part of herself that day. I said, "No!" I couldn't trust her anymore. What would stop her from hurting me like that again in the future?

Every night that week she called me and begged me to take her back, but I refused. At the end of the week, she called me hysterically crying. She was screaming crying. I had never heard anyone cry like that before, and I couldn't handle hearing her in so much pain. I said, "Okay, okay, calm down, calm down, everything is going to be okay. I will take you back."

Nancy treated me better than ever after that. Eventually I started to trust her again, and our relationship went back to the way it was before. A few weeks after we got back together, I had to go to North Carolina for a family reunion. It was 1993, and cell phones were unheard of back then. The only way we could talk was for her to call the hotel. She was supposed to call on Tuesday evening and then again on Thursday evening between four and six p.m. Thursday was special because it was our anniversary.

My whole family went out to the beach on Tuesday night, but I waited in the hotel for Nancy to call. She never did. This really hurt me, but I gave her the benefit of the doubt. Thursday came, and I waited for her to call. Four o'clock came and went. Five o'clock came and went. Six o'clock came and went. Six thirty rolled around, and I started to get restless. Everyone was preparing to leave for a special family dinner, and I absolutely had to go. A half-hour before we left, my aunt saw that something was wrong and started to ask me questions. I explained a little of the situation to her. She lent me her calling card, so that I could call Nancy before we had to leave.

Nancy answered the phone when I called. It turned out that she was home babysitting her two little brothers the whole time. This really upset me because there was no reason for her not to call me. She was acting very indifferent toward me, and didn't seem to care about me at all. She then delivered an unexpected surprise and broke up with me *again*! It turned out that her old boyfriend was hanging around the whole time I was away. It was a situation of, "Out of sight, out of mind." Once again, I was deeply hurt; only this time I was really angry too. I was angry with myself for taking her back and trusting her.

After I hung up the phone, I sat in the room with the door closed and the lights out feeling filled with anger, confusion, and pain. I cried out in agony, "Why God? WHY?" Just then, something unexpected happened. I did not hear a voice with my ears, but a strong message from God literally *shot* into my head like a bullet. I am not exaggerating when I say, "shot like a bullet" because it physically almost knocked me over. His answer to my question was, "NOW YOU LEARNED YOUR LESSON!" The moment I heard those words, I could feel in my soul that God was intensely angry with me. He also filled me with a complete understanding of why sex outside of marriage is wrong. Before that happened, I never understood *why* it was so wrong. My teachers never explained the reason *why*. They just told us we were not supposed to do it.

I now understood that sex creates an incredibly strong bond between two people. God made it this way to cement marriages together. God wants this bond to make marriages strong and unbreakable so that married couples can endure all the trials that life has to offer. Sex creates a spiritual and emotional connection that is not designed to be broken. Through having sex with Nancy, my soul was actually united to hers. The reason why breaking up felt like a large part of my soul was literally ripped away from me was because that is exactly what happened. God's teachings, given through the Catholic Church, are not telling us to save sex for marriage because they want to take away our fun. They give us this teaching so that we don't destroy ourselves. I never realized that the reason behind this teaching was largely to protect me from getting hurt.

The bond that sex creates is like using super glue to permanently attach something to the skin on your arm. If you decide to rip it off once the glue has dried, your flesh is going to tear off with it. It is going to cause major damage and a massive amount of pain. You are going to bleed a lot, and it is going to take a long time to heal.

I told God I was sorry for my sin. I promised Him that I would not have sex again until I was married. I just hoped that someone would still want to marry me since I had lost my virginity. It made me feel like "damaged goods." I began to wonder how I ever got so far off track. I thought I was really over all the hard stuff in life. I thought I was going to just keep getting better and better as a person until I died and went to heaven. Obviously, I was wrong. Motivated by the pain in my heart, I began to refocus. I started asking myself again at the end of each day, "If I would have died today, would I have gone to heaven?" I made every effort to live in such a way that I could confidently answer *yes* to that question.

PART THREE—The Beginning of My College Days

FIRST SEMESTER AT PENN STATE

Not long after Nancy dumped me, I had the first of three mouth surgeries for getting permanent teeth. This first procedure was a bone graft surgery that left me in a lot of pain for the rest of the summer. I'll spare you the details.

The one thing that made me feel better about my overall life situation was the thought of starting college. I viewed college as a brand new start in life. No one would know me or have any preconceived ideas of who I was as a person. I was hoping that everyone would like me. College would be a chance to make good friends and do more of the things I liked to do. I would be able to decide how I would spend most of my time. I would no longer be trapped in school all day or have restrictions at home.

The first experience I had at my branch campus of Penn State was orientation week. Meeting new people was a lot of fun, but my most vivid memory is how I totally humiliated myself by the end of the week. There was one guy in my dorm whose name was Jim. I was coming back from dinner at the cafeteria when I saw him standing outside of our dorm talking to a very pretty girl. I started saying in a silly sounding voice, "The Jim mannn, the Jiminator, Jimolaaa…" I was doing this to imitate a *Saturday Night Live* skit that was very popular at that time. I thought I was being funny and cool. Every time I saw him throughout the rest of the week I called him "The Jim Man" or "The Jimanator" using the same silly voice.

Jim stopped me at the end of the week, put his hand on my shoulder, looked me in the eyes and said, "I don't know how to tell you this but…" He paused, looked down at the ground, then looked back up at me and said…"My name's not Jim… It's Joe." Ohhhh mannnnn! How embarrassing! I wanted to crawl under a rock and die! For the rest of the year, Joe called me "The Jim Man" or "The Jimanator" every time he saw me.

Aside from totally humiliating myself, I spent all my time hanging out with my new friends. It was a lot of fun because classes hadn't started yet, so none of us had a single responsibility. We would stay up making jokes and enjoying ourselves until the early hours of morning. Even after classes started, we would hang out until late at night making each other laugh.

For the first month or two of school, my friends and I stayed pretty clean. We figured that no one was drinking alcohol because it was only a two year campus, and no one was twenty-one yet. It was also a designated dry campus, which meant alcohol was not permitted. My perception changed when I went into the sophomore's dorm room next to mine. Their room was completely loaded with empty alcohol bottles. They told me that they had been drinking every night since the first week of school. This shocked me. Suddenly, a bottle of gin appeared. Without giving it much thought, I drank some of it with them. Deep down I knew I wasn't supposed to drink alcohol, but I didn't let myself think before acting. I didn't want to miss out on all the fun. I wanted to be able to drink without worrying if it was right or wrong. The bottom line is that I compromised my moral beliefs *again*.

I encourage you to never compromise your moral convictions for any reason! It will only come back to bite you later on. After all I had been through, I should have chosen more wisely. I hope you will not make the same mistakes I made.

Although I had compromised on this belief, I still wanted to be the best person I could be in other areas of my life. One way I felt I could still be a good person was to go to Church on Sunday even though no one around me was going. Virtually no one even talked about it. I drove around the area for hours looking for a Catholic Church but never found one. I just kept getting lost and frustrated. I looked in the phone book but didn't find any Catholic Churches. After my unsuccessful effort to find a Church, I concluded that it was not my fault that I wasn't making it to Church on Sunday.

UNEXPECTED WAKEUP CALL

I hesitate to tell you about this next thing that happened. I'm afraid you will think I'm crazy because of what I experienced. To be honest, I think a lot of people have experiences like this one, but they are afraid to admit it to themselves or anyone else. Like me, they don't want people to think they are crazy, or perhaps they just don't have enough faith to believe it can happen.

I was alone sitting Indian style on the floor of my dorm room. It was night time and very quiet. I looked down on the floor next to me. The first and only necklace I had ever bought was there. It was an iron cross on a chain. I always had a fascination with crosses, which is why I bought the necklace at my Church's Christmas Bazaar when I was in sixth grade.

As I looked at the cross necklace on the floor, I thought to myself, "How did that get here? I know I left it hanging on the wall in my bedroom at home." The chain *literally* began to move the moment I finished asking that question. Startled by the movement of the chain, I immediately sprang onto my hands and knees. I was mesmerized and puzzled by what I was seeing. I thought to myself, "WOW! This is like being in a movie or something. How is it moving?" As the chain moved, I could hear the metallic jingle sound that a chain makes when being bounced around in your hand. The chain continued to move around until it came to rest in the form of an ankh-shaped cross, which is a cross with a loop at the top. It was an Egyptian symbol for eternal life and has been used in the Orthodox Church. The whole situation had me dumbfounded. Then the chain, remaining in the ankh-shaped cross pattern, started sliding across the floor. It continued to make the metallic jingling sound as it rustled across the rough carpet. I crawled after it, unable to process any thought. I just couldn't believe what was happening! The chain hit my closet door, making a loud chain-crunching sound, and stopped.

An eerie silence fell over the room. Then a sound like an explosive, erupting, mighty, volcanic, thunderous wind completely engulfed the building. It was beyond intense! It was louder than my human capacity could handle, yet somehow it didn't hurt my ears at all. The sound was filled with power. It went right through me as if I wasn't even there. It lifted me straight up off the floor, and I reacted with a loud scream. I frantically tried to grab hold of something to keep myself from floating up any higher. The only thing I could reach was a small brown metal trash can. I quickly grabbed it and hugged it tightly, hoping that the weight of it would help hold me down. My body slowly rotated as I floated upward until I was completely upside down. When I was about twelve feet off the floor, I realized that the trash can was not helping me, so I let it go. Gravity pulled it back down, and it made a loud crashing noise as it collided with the floor. I was surprised that I could even hear the metal can hit the floor because the loud, deafening, thunderous sound continued to engulf me.

The next thing I knew, the building had completely disappeared. I was totally surrounded by an empty black chasm as I continued to float upward. It wasn't an absolute black, but a light shade of black, interspersed with streams of hazy gray.

I cannot even put into words how petrified I was by this entire event! I didn't know what was going on, but I wondered if I was dying. I didn't want to die. There were so many things I wanted to accomplish in my life. I started yelling out, "Please! Please God! Please! Please let me stay! Please let me stay!" Suddenly I stopped ascending and simultaneously stopped begging God to let me stay. I immediately began to descend back down toward the earth.

The building reappeared, and I found myself floating across my dorm room about four feet off the floor. I circled halfway around the room and then over top of my bed. As soon as my body was over the bed, the ear-piercing, volcanic noise suddenly stopped as my eyes jolted open. I found myself lying motionless in my bed filled with intense panic and fear from what had just happened. My heart was pounding profusely! I quickly glanced over at the clock and saw that it was around two in the morning.

The room was filled with an incredibly eerie silence. In a loud, clear voice, I suddenly heard the word "Dad." The moment I heard it, I knew within myself that it was God the Father, my "Dad," who had just visited me. The word "Dad" had come out of my roommate's mouth as he slept. He didn't move or make any other noises. He just spoke that one word loudly and clearly. He *never* talked in his sleep before or after that night. I nervously said my roommate's name out loud to see if he was awake, but he didn't respond. I lay there perfectly still because I was afraid to move. It was so silent that it didn't seem normal. This amplified the utterly creepy feeling that already pervaded my soul. I knew there was no chance I was going to fall back to sleep because I am a sensitive sleeper to begin with. Being completely filled with fear left me with no chance of falling back to sleep. I then said, "God, there is no way I am going to be able to fall back to sleep because I am so afraid right now. Please let me fall back to sleep." In what seemed like the blink of an eye, my alarm clock was going off the next morning.

The moment my eyes opened I deeply realized what had happened to me the night before. A massive smile immediately came over my face. I felt so happy and yelled, "WOW! GOD VISITED ME LAST NIGHT!" It made me feel special to think that God would actually come and visit me like that. I thought He was going to start visiting me every night, which made me want to get myself back to Church. "If God is going to be visiting me, I need to prepare myself," I thought. I resolved to drive home every weekend and go to Church with my parents, since I never found a Catholic Church near the school.

The night after this first visit I went to bed with intense excitement because I expected God to visit me again. The excitement made it difficult for me to fall asleep, but I eventually did. The following morning I woke up and realized that nothing had happened. Days passed, and I waited for my second visit. Weeks passed, but He still had not come.

TURBULENT ENDING

Over the next few months, I continued to drive home for Mass every weekend, but my fervor eventually faded. My life was taking on a much different feel than it had when I first started college. A side effect from driving home for Mass every weekend was that I wasn't around to hang out with my friends on the weekends. I also was not spending as much time with them during the week because my classes were harder the second semester. I needed to spend more time studying in order to maintain my grade point average. The end result was that my friends started to resent me. They started talking about me behind my back and pushing me out of their lives. This was painful for me. I was trying to do the right thing by going home for Church and focusing on my grades, but I was paying a painful price for it.

One other significant event that dramatically impacted my social life was my second mouth surgery that I had over spring break. It was an excruciatingly painful tissue graft surgery. They cut a thick chunk of skin from the roof of my mouth and stitched it to the front of my upper gums. The pain was so bad that for the first time in my life, I actually wanted to die. I also was not allowed to wear my dentures for over a month while my mouth healed. As a result, I avoided talking because I didn't want anyone to find out that I didn't have real teeth.

On one occasion, I completely failed to hide my secret. A girl that I liked was walking in front of me down the hallway. She asked me a question, then turned back to look at me while I responded. The moment I answered, her eyes opened wide, and her jaw dropped in disbelief. She obviously was shocked. While she was dealing with the realization that my mouth looked like a black hole, I was dealing with the utter humiliation of the fact that she now knew my secret. I watched as her mind unsuccessfully tried to process what she had just seen. She attempted to formulate a question or a statement but was unable to. The only thing that came out of her mouth was, "Uh, um, that, you, I, um." I was embarrassed that she found out, but I was so emotionally worn out by the whole situation that I just didn't care anymore. I explained what happened, and she went away feeling shocked.

Socially, my school year continued to go downhill. I became so psychologically numb that I completely forgot about the spiritual experience I had in the beginning of the year.

About a month and a half before summer, things began to turn in my favor. I met a *very* pretty girl who lived near my parent's house. She dated me even though I didn't have teeth, which surprised me. I really liked her a *lot*! All the guys in my dorm asked me how I got such a pretty girl to go out with me. I could tell they were hoping to gain some special insight that might help them enhance their own dating lives. I never had a good answer for them because I couldn't understand why she was with me either.

I was ready to do anything necessary to keep her in my life. This influenced me to make many bad choices. I did whatever I thought she wanted, rather than what I knew was right. It was like total self-destruction. I sinned in all the ways I didn't want to.

She suddenly and unexpectedly stopped talking to me near the end of the school year. The breakup of our relationship devastated me. It happened a week before final exams which made studying nearly impossible. I felt like my world was completely falling apart.

My life had become such a mess. I felt I was not prepared for the independence associated with college life, especially all the social decisions I had to make. At the end of my freshman year, I remember thinking, "When I was finishing high school, I thought I had everything figured out in life. Now I realize I have *nothing* figured out!"

SUMMER

During the summer I had my next mouth surgery. This was the first of the dental implant procedures. I will warn you now. If you are a person who does not deal well with blood and pain, skip ahead to the next section without reading any more of this one.

The surgery started out the same as the bone graft and tissue graft procedures had. The surgeon pumped a ton of local anesthetic into my gums and the roof of my mouth. I absolutely *hated* every second of it! I was squirming in the chair as that big metal needle plunged into the sensitive areas of my mouth. I felt the Novocain fluid get pumped into the blood vessels underneath my skin.

After I was numbed up, the surgeon cut me open. I didn't feel pain, but I could feel the cool blade run all the way through my gums from one side of my mouth to the other. I could hear the noise of my skin being sliced open as the scalpel slid through it. Blood flooded into my mouth and throat as he sliced.

After he clamped the flesh of my gums out of the way, the surgeon brought out the first of two different drills and began to drill into my upper jawbone. The first drill sounded much like the kind they use for drilling out cavities. It had a high-pitched squeal. The second was a low-pitched, loud, rumbling drill like the kind a carpenter uses to drill through wood. This drill made my whole head shake and vibrate as it thrashed through my bone. I could see smoke and smell the odor of grease and something burning as he drilled into my head. My absolute hatred for this situation intensified with each passing second, and I am painfully squirming in my chair as I relive it now by writing about it for you!

In spite of the Novocain, I was feeling a torturous level of pain. Halfway through the procedure, the pain became so intense that I couldn't bear it anymore. Every time I yelled, the doctor stopped and pumped more Novocain into me but it didn't help. I could see the confusion on his face. He didn't know what to do. I was awake and coherent, but I stopped responding to him. The pain had exceeded my maximum threshold.

My mind completely shut down. I didn't care about anything anymore. I could have just died right then and there as far as I was concerned. I was told later that I turned a deathly shade of white. I observed a helpless panic overtake the surgeon's face. He and his team stopped operating, sat me up in the chair, and started fanning me to get more air in my face. I was aware that they were talking to me and asking me questions, but I didn't respond. I just sat there motionless and in pain. They realized that they had no choice but to finish the surgery, so they lay me back down, and he continued drilling.

I was told later that the bone he packed in during the bone graft surgery had partially closed off my nasal passages. He had to drill out my nasal passages in addition to drilling holes in my jaw for the metal implant sleeves. When all the drilling was finished, and the metal sleeves were in place, they stretched my gums back over the bone and the new metal pieces and then stitched me back together.

I spent the first half of that summer sitting on my butt trying to recover. I wasted most of my time playing computer golf and trying to get better at playing the guitar. The second half of summer was a little better. I worked as an archery instructor at a summer day camp, which was a nice experience.

Toward the end of the summer I attended a week long training session at college, so that I could serve as a campus tour guide during the upcoming school year. One of our first major duties was to help with the freshman orientation week. All the guys were excited about this because it meant we would be the first ones to see all the new freshman girls. All in all my summer flew by, and I found myself packing to leave for my second year of college.

As I previously mentioned, I learned a lot about being on my own during my first year at college. I was anxious to apply my new ideas to deal with various life situations in my sophomore year. One of the major decisions I made before going back to school was that I was *not* going to get into any serious relationships that year. I figured it would be smarter just to focus on my studies and get the best grades I could in order to prepare for my future.

NO WAY!

Everyone was talking about Samantha, the beautiful girl from Spain, throughout the whole week of freshman orientation. She was fairly tall with blond hair, blue eyes, and an amazingly attractive accent. Just seeing her and hearing her voice challenged my idea of avoiding a serious relationship that year.

Samantha ended up being in my Calculus class. I couldn't help but look for her every time I got there. About a month into the school year, I arrived at class, slid my skateboard under my desk, and then slowly raised my head to see that she was sitting down in the seat next to me. Excitedly, I thought to myself, "HELLO!" Even though I was totally aware of her presence, I tried to make it seem like I didn't even notice her. The teacher started class, but Samantha had my full attention. I wanted to do something to impress her.

Not many people knew I had been growing my hair long because I kept it pulled up under my cap most of the time. I decided to take my hat off and let my hair slide down the sides of my face. Then I slowly ran my fingers through it a few times. After I thought she had a good look, I pushed it back up under my hat. Throughout this process, I did my best to make it look like I wasn't even thinking about what I was doing. I'm laughing at myself now as I look back and write about my actions.

My little display must have worked. After class, Samantha started talking to me. As she spoke, I was thinking, "NO WAY! I can't believe SHEEEE is talking to MEEEE!" We walked to another classroom building and talked the whole way. I didn't want to miss my opportunity, so I asked for her phone number before I left for my next class. She was quick to give it to me. As I walked away from our encounter, I couldn't help but smile. I was so excited!

We talked on the phone that night. A day or two later she came to visit me between classes at my dorm room. We sat on my couch and talked. After a while, I put on my favorite slow song. In a very slick way, I asked her to dance. She accepted with a smile. There I was in my dorm room dancing with the girl that everyone was talking about! It took all my energy to hold back my smile. After the song, she excused herself to use the bathroom. I just stood there, amazed at what was happening. As soon as she came back, she said, "Well, I have to be going to my next class now." Her breath reeked of mouthwash. I took this to mean only one thing; she wanted to kiss me. So without any hesitation, I stepped up and kissed her. Just like that, our relationship began.

A MAJOR LIFE LESSON

One of the most memorable lessons of my life happened while I was going out Samantha. We had a major argument about two months into our relationship. I was very mad at her and wanted her to apologize to me. Somehow she thought I was the one at fault. Our conflict carried on from the morning to the early afternoon.

Later that day, I was lying on my bed looking up at the top bunk, thinking about the whole situation. A thought gently came to my mind: "What if she is right and I am wrong?" Being wrong never occurred to me as being possible before because I always knew when I was right. I then turned the situation around and looked at it from her perspective. I assumed she was right, and I was completely at fault. I was shocked at what I saw. For the first time in my life, I realized that it *was* my fault! Until that moment, I was unable to clearly see or admit when I was wrong about something because I was never willing to think it was even possible. Looking at the whole situation from both our perspectives enabled me to see that we were both at fault. This may not sound like much on paper, but it was a major life lesson for me. I learned how to look at a situation from someone else's standpoint before assuming that they were wrong and I was right. I also learned how to admit and accept the ways that I can be wrong.

Ever since that day, I have made it a personal discipline to double-check myself every time a conflict arises in one of my relationships. I take an honest look and consider if it is my fault instead of jumping to conclusions and automatically assuming that the other person is to blame. This single lesson significantly shaped the person I am today. I strongly encourage you to apply this concept in your own life the next time you think you are right and someone else is completely wrong.

Samantha and I talked about what happened, and we both apologized. I felt like we were mature, and this gave me a lot of hope for our future. We worked at our relationship harder than any relationship I had ever been in before. I think it was because we both desperately wanted it to work.

Even though we both tried hard, we had many ups and downs. Her way of thinking was very different from mine, which made *all* of our communication extremely difficult. We stayed together for a large part of the school year. We tried to hold on to the relationship as long as we could. In the end, we were both so emotionally worn out that we mutually decided to split up.

This relationship took so much out of me that I decided I was not going to get into another one for a long time. I spared you the details, but I did slack off on my moral convictions in this relationship. This made the recovery process even more difficult to handle when it was over.

SMILE

Near the end of the school year, I had my last mouth surgery. All they had to do was expose the metal sleeves they had put in my upper jaw, screw caps on them, and trim my gums out of the way a little bit. After that, I was fitted with my permanent teeth. A porcelain plate that looks like real teeth was bolted into the metal sleeves that the surgeon had implanted in my upper jaw. This enabled me to bite into things like apples and hard pretzels again. I would no longer have to soak my teeth in a cup at night or glue them in every morning. I didn't have to worry about people finding out that my teeth were only a piece of removable plastic. I wouldn't have to worry about getting embarrassed from my dentures coming loose and sliding partly out of my mouth while I was talking. I was also very grateful to be done with all the surgeries. I don't think anyone at that age should have to deal with those kinds of worries. I hope I never have to go through anything like that again!

FINALLY! THIS IS THE ONE!

The school year ended, and I took two weeks off before I started my summer environmental internship. I was very excited about this job. I wanted to make a good impression on my first day, so I went to bed early the night before. Not long after I got in bed, my bedroom door flew open and someone turned on the light. It was Steve. We had been in the same class from fifth all the way through twelfth grade. Walking in behind Steve was Kim. She had been a grade below us in high school. I hadn't seen her for two years. I had wanted to date her in high school, but it had never worked out. She had always ended up in a relationship with someone else before I had a chance to ask her out.

My long hair fell down across my face as I sat up in bed. They came in and sat down. The three of us joked and talked for about forty-five minutes. When they were leaving, Kim looked back at me and enticingly said, "Give me a call some time!" This was very exciting for me. The look in her eyes really added to the flavor of the situation.

I really enjoyed Kim's company that evening. We joked around very well together. I decided to call her on Friday night before she left to go babysitting. At the end of the week, I did as I had planned.

We seemed to "click" in a big way! Both of us had changed since high school, and we seemed to fit perfectly together now. We started dating a week later. This relationship was so much different from the last one I was in. Everything went so smoothly and seemed to flow very naturally between us. We even went to Mass together every Sunday. I started thinking about the house and kids.

I really wanted this relationship to work out, and I wanted to do things right. I told Kim I wanted to save myself for marriage and not get physically involved in any way. She accepted my request, but didn't like it because she didn't want to "put any restrictions on our relationship." I knew that sex created an incredibly strong bond. I had already learned my lesson as to why it is wrong, so I stood firm in my decision that we should wait.

The thing that set this relationship apart from all the others was that I had a deep feeling inside of me. Somehow I just knew that being with her was right. I had never felt more sure about anything in my entire life. Asking Kim to marry me seemed like the right thing to do. I thought about it for a long time and decided to wait a year before I asked her. I still had two years of college, and she had three. I was turning twenty-one, and she was turning twenty. We were still young, so it seemed sensible to wait until the end of the year.

The very next time I saw Kim, I just couldn't hold back. I started talking about my thoughts. She felt the same way, and everything seemed so right! As we sat there looking up at the stars, I decided to propose. She immediately accepted with a big smile.

The one thing I always longed for in life was to be married. Her yes made me incredibly happy. It felt like a dream come true! We decided to wait until the end of the upcoming school year before getting an official engagement ring and telling our families. In the meantime, I gave her my crucifix ring. I had worn it for four years without taking it off. I had planned to wear it until I met the girl I was going to marry, and then give it to her as a symbolic gift. We planned to view it as our undercover engagement ring until the end of the year.

DREADING A LONG DISTANCE RELATIONSHIP

It was by far the best summer of my life. Kim and I did everything together. I found myself head-over-heels in love with her. One of the many things I did for her was to secretly write about our relationship every single day in a notebook journal. I carefully recorded all of the things we did together and how I felt about her. After I filled the first book, I gave it to her on her birthday and started a new one.

As the summer was coming to an end, I prepared myself for a difficult year ahead. Our schools were three hours apart. I didn't like the thought of being away from Kim. I was petrified of losing her. Somewhere along the way I started thinking about the strong but forbidden bond that I had experienced in the past. I started *rationalizing* and making excuses like: "I love her. I am going to marry her. What is the difference if we start now or later? We are *definitely* going to get married anyway. It's not like I am sleeping around. She doesn't think it is necessary for us to wait, so why should we?" It didn't take long to convince myself that it was okay for us to have sex. I came to believe that I needed to do it in order to make sure she would be faithful to me while we were away at school. I thought it would bring us closer together and make our relationship stronger and unbreakable.

After you finish this book, I encourage you to come back and study the thought patterns I had in this section. Also go back and study the thoughts I had after sinning with Nancy the first time. Train yourself to recognize when you are thinking this way in your own mind. It could be on a different topic, but the *rationalizing* thought process will be similar.

A good way to neutralize the *rationalization* is to ask yourself, "If I go through with this, and then die five minutes later, will I make it to heaven?" Be perfectly honest with yourself and listen to your conscience. Even though it may seem difficult, it is in your best interest to *go against rationalizing* thoughts that lead to sin.

KICK IT

My junior year of college was also going to be my first year at the main campus of Penn State. I was really looking forward to getting away from the small branch campus and being at the large main campus.

Two days before I left for school, one of my friends was having a going-back-to-school party. Kim and I went together. A number of people were swimming in his big in-ground pool. They kept bugging me to join them. I didn't feel like swimming, but after a while I started to give in to their constant badgering. I snuck into the house and changed into my bathing suit without telling anyone.

It was ten o'clock at night and pitch black outside. The only light was inside the pool under the diving board. I decided to make a surprise cannonball entrance into the pool, so I bolted across the yard at top speed. Because it was so dark, I couldn't see that the concrete sidewalk around the pool stuck up about four inches higher than the grass. While I was still at full stride, my foot connected with the concrete like a kicker punting a football. A scream roared out of my mouth as I fell flat on my face in excruciating pain.

Fortunately for me, the sidewalk was only four feet wide. My face made it to the pool, but my stomach and legs scraped across the concrete, peeling skin off as I went. My whole body sank as I screamed in agony under the water. There were a lot of people in the pool, but only a few of them saw what happened. It took all my effort to hide the pain I was in. I climbed out of the pool and limped over to the house. Kim came over to see what had happened. She helped me cover the bleeding areas and then took me home. My parents helped by putting ice on my foot after I got onto my bed, but it didn't seem to make much of a difference. I was in agony!

My aunt took me to the doctor the following morning. The x-ray showed that I had blasted the middle bone in my big toe into five pieces. My family doctor immediately sent me to a specialist at a nearby hospital. We drove there and waited for an hour only to find out that there wasn't anything he could do for it. He just taped my big toe to the one next to it and made me buy a special boot-like shoe. It would prevent me from bending my toes. The boot was the ugliest looking thing I had ever seen! It was diarrhea brown in color with a chunk of plywood for a sole. The front was wide open, which made my unsightly, bruised, swollen toes visible to everyone. This was going to make for an embarrassing start to my first year at the main campus.

FIRST SEMESTER, PHONE TIME

The year was 1995. Cell phones were still virtually unheard of, and all the long-distance calling plans charged a lot of money for each minute of use. I wasn't working during the school year because I needed to devote all my spare time to studying in order to keep my grades up. I also had to pay my rent, car insurance, and other bills with the money I had saved over the summer.

Because of these budget factors, Kim and I had to limit our phone conversations to just twenty minutes a day. Twenty minutes went by fast. It just wasn't enough time. It seemed like we would get on the phone and have to say goodbye in the next breath. The other thing that was difficult was that we'd spend all day looking forward to talking with each other, but when we were finally on the phone, we couldn't think of what to say. The whole situation was a serious strain on our relationship.

Kim created a rule early in the school year that we both agreed to. She made me promise that the last thing we would say to each other before hanging up the phone was, "I love you!" No matter what happened, or what was said in the conversation, "I love you" had to be the last words we spoke to each other before hanging up.

Whatever I forgot or didn't get to tell her in our phone conversations, I wrote about in the notebook journal that I continued to write in *every day* for her. Whereas the first one focused on things we did together, this one was an expression of what my life was like while we were away from each other, and how I thought about her constantly in everything I did.

TOE

I was grateful that my toe was broken when the weekends rolled around. My injury prevented me from being able to go to any parties for the first six weeks of school. The best part about this was that I didn't have to deal with being pressured by my roommates or friends to go out partying with them.

The way I saw it, guys went to parties to get drunk and try to pick up girls. I didn't want to do either one. I just wanted to be focused on my fiancé and my schoolwork.

REVISITED

This next event happened about a month into the new school year. I had come home from class and laid down on my bed because I was tired. While staring at the poster above my roommate's bed, I thought, "How in the world can he like that band so much?" Then suddenly, it came like a volcanic eruption. It was the same ear-piercing, all-consuming, thunderous sound that I had experienced during my first year of college on the night God the Father visited me. The explosive sound went right through me and exhilarated every nerve ending in my entire being. It was beyond intense! I was totally aware of every single nerve ending in my entire body all at the same time. I felt weightless and ecstatic and wished that it would never end. I floated straight up from my bed and began ascending. The building completely disappeared, and I was surrounded by a blackish, grayish tunnel-like chasm just like the first time.

As you can recall, I ascended upside down the first time this happened. This time, I immediately went into a kneeling position with my hands folded in prayer and floated up headfirst. I then sincerely prayed, "Lord, if this is my time, please, just let me be ready." Then I started to feel a little curious. I decided to try peeking upward to see where I was going and what it looked like. I slowly began to raise my head. Before I was able to look high enough to see anything, I stopped ascending and began to descend. My body continued to feel utterly exhilarated the entire time, and the thunderously loud, ear-piercing rumble continued throughout the experience.

The next thing I knew, I was back in my apartment bedroom. I floated around the room then over top of my bed. The moment my body was over the bed my eyes slammed open, and I was lying there staring at my roommate's poster.

The whole experience was so physical and real. It engaged every one of my senses to the utmost capacity. I was happy when I realized how I responded this time. The first time this happened I was utterly petrified and begged God to let me stay on earth. This time I went into a prayer stance and asked God to let me be ready for heaven. After the first visit, I made an effort to get back to Church every Sunday. It was possible because I could drive home to my parents, which was only an hour away. This time I was three hours away, and I couldn't drive home every weekend for Mass.

I had already driven around the whole town looking for a Catholic Church but didn't find one. I looked in the phone book but was still unsuccessful. Since I couldn't find a Church, I focused on making more of an effort to say my prayers before going to sleep at night.

It wasn't until years later that I learned why I had not been able to find any Catholic Churches in the phone books. I always looked for the words "Catholic Church," but they were *not* listed under "Catholic Church" in the phone books I was using. They were listed under "ROMAN Catholic Church."

ROUGH SEMESTER

During that semester, I joined the Penn State Archery Club. This gave me a chance to be around people who were interested in something that I really enjoyed. Everything else in my life seemed to be getting more difficult, especially my relationship with Kim. She kept backing out of plans we made. I would pack up my things and call her just before walking out the door to go visit her. She would then tell me to not come. Her usual excuse was that she had too much homework. This really hurt me! She also wasn't calling me as much, and she frequently wasn't around to take my calls. I knew that I had to trust her if things were going to work out, but it was becoming increasingly difficult to do. She didn't seem as willing to go out of her way for me as I was for her. I hoped she was being faithful, but she was *not* making me feel very reassured about it. In November, Kim and I talked about the fact that she wasn't calling me. After a heated discussion, she apologized and agreed to try harder.

That night some of my friends nagged me to go out to a frat party with them. I went, but the fraternity brothers would not let us in because they were only letting girls in. This didn't bother me at all. I went straight home so that I could call Kim. I was excited that she seemed more willing to work at our relationship, and I wanted to talk to her some more. When I got to my apartment, I quickly dialed her number and waited anxiously to hear her soft voice. A smile came over my face as I heard the phone get picked up. My smile immediately disappeared when some strange guy said, "Hello." I asked for Kim, and he put her on the phone. The fact that a guy was in her room at midnight on a Saturday deeply bothered me! In addition to that, she seemed reluctant to talk to me. Since she wasn't saying anything, I said, "Well, I guess I'll let you go." I was hoping that she would say "No," and then make more of an effort in our conversation. Instead, she said, "Okay," and then hung up.

My adrenaline immediately went through the roof! She didn't say, "I love you!" It was her rule, and she didn't say it! I redialed her number at lightning speed. I assured myself that nothing could be going on because her little sister was supposed to be there for the weekend. That was the reason she had given me when she said I couldn't visit her. She answered after several rings. I reminded her of our little rule that *she* had made up. I told her I really needed to hear her say she loved me. Instead, she just hung up on me. Then my anger and hurt emotions exploded uncontrollably! With intense fury and trembling hands, I redialed. Kim answered the phone, got mad at me for calling again, and then hung up on me.

I stormed around my bedroom filled with intense, explosive rage! It took all my effort to keep from destroying everything in sight! I was in a dangerous emotional state. After pacing for a long time, I partially calmed down and tried calling again. This time there was no answer. I didn't know what to do with myself. I eventually tried going to bed, but I was unable to sleep.

My mind was filled with unnerving thoughts about the guy that was in her dorm room and what could possibly be going on. After a while, I took my notebook journal out and started writing. Lying in my bed, I wrote a seventeen page entry about how I had trusted Kim and how much she had hurt me. Although I didn't want our relationship to end, it was time to break up. If it was meant to be, then maybe we would get back together some day. It took me well over an hour to write everything down. After I had finished, and got it all out of my system, I fell asleep.

Writing everything out on paper helped me tremendously, and I recommend it to anyone who is in a lot of emotional pain.

I was still lying in bed when the phone rang around nine o'clock the next morning. It was Kim. She was crying and apologized for the way she acted. I told her about the long journal entry

I made during the night and that I was planning to end our relationship. She said, "I understand that you want to break up with me, but I am asking you for another chance. I promise I will make it up to you and try harder. I love you. I thought about what happened last night and realized that I couldn't bear the thought of losing you. Please don't break up with me." I asked her about the guy that answered the phone. She told me that he was just passing by to say, "Hi" at the time of my call. She assured me that nothing was going on between them. I loved her so much that I was willing to stay with her and work at our relationship.

My relationship with Kim was wonderful for the next two weeks. She called me all the time and was there to take my calls when she said she would be. This made me so happy. As December approached, Kim unfortunately started to regress in her efforts. I was supposed to go visit her the week before finals. She canceled our plans as she had done every other time for the past month. She gave me the same reason as before. She had too much homework. This really disappointed me. To compensate for this cancellation, we made plans for the day she came home for Christmas break. She was finished with her final exams on Thursday. I was finished with mine on Friday morning. She would be dropped off at her parent's house around five o'clock on Saturday. She would call me the moment she got in the door, and I would drive straight over to see her. This plan made me feel a little better and gave me something to look forward to.

This is what I looked like during this stage of my life.

THE TRAGIC CALL

My dad called me at nine o'clock in the morning on the first day of finals week. This was the first time he had ever called me at college. I immediately knew something bad had happened. His voice made it even more obvious that something was wrong. With a concerned, firm yell, I asked, "WHAT'S UP DAD?" He told me to sit down. I remained standing and nervously yelled, "WHAT'S GOING ON DAD?" He paused, and then responded, "Your little cousin Jerry died this morning." I was stunned. Jerry was only twelve years old. He was a great kid and an amazing athlete. He won numerous first place championship titles in wrestling and placed within the top four in the National wrestling tournament every year. He was also the MVP on his first place championship baseball team. We were all so proud of him. Not only was he an amazing athlete; he was one of the most lovable kids I knew! I yelled, "WHAT HAPPENED?" My dad replied, "He had an asthma attack and didn't make it."

Neither of us spoke for a few moments, and then he said, "Sean, your Great Grandmother died this morning too." In shock and disbelief, I yelled, "WHAT HAPPENED?" "She died of natural causes," he replied. He went on to say that the funeral for my Great Grandmother was Friday morning. I had my last final exam that morning, so I couldn't even be there. The viewing for Jerry was Friday night, and his funeral was on Saturday morning. I was relieved that I could at least make it to his viewing and funeral. Our conversation ended, and I stood there upset and speechless.

After I regained some composure, I called Kim hoping to get some support from her. I told her what happened. I also said I could pick her up on my way home on Friday so that she could be there with me. Even though she was finished with her finals on Thursday, she refused. She said that she had plans with her friends on Friday and couldn't break them. It destroyed me to hear her say that. In a surprised and strained voice I said, "What? I would be there for you!" She got mad at me for saying that and responded, "Well I'm not you," and then ended our conversation.

Later that day, I sat down to study but it seemed pointless. I could not concentrate. After one day of living in complete turmoil, I realized that I needed to come up with a way to deal with the situation in order to make it through the week. I said to myself, "Okay, there is nothing I can do about my relationship with Kim or the funerals while I am here. I must try to put those things aside until I am home. Right now I *must* focus all of my energy on getting through these finals. Worrying all week about something I have no control over will not do me any good."

On Wednesday night, my old friend Matt called. We hadn't spoken in about four years. It was a surprise to hear from him. I figured my worried mother had put him up to it. He asked me if I was still playing the guitar. I answered, "Yeah, a little." He then invited me over to his house on Friday night to "hang out and jam" in his band room. I accepted, and told him I would call him around nine o'clock in the evening when I got home from my cousin's viewing.

I called Kim every single night of finals week, but she was never there and didn't return a single one of my phone calls. It felt like I had the weight of the world on my shoulders: death, final exams, and the girl I was in love with was ignoring me when I needed her the most.

On Thursday night, I laid in bed filled with anxiety as I stared at the ceiling tiles. A million thoughts ran through my mind. I didn't get a single second of sleep that night. At eight o'clock the following morning, I took my last exam, loaded up my car, and then drove home.

THE VIEWING

The viewing for my cousin was very emotional. I stood there for hours with my arm around my uncle and bawled my eyes out. Every single time I looked down at my cousin, I would get worse. Seeing his lifeless, pale, cold body lying in the casket tore me apart both inside and out. I was powerless against the sorrow and anguish it made me feel. The viewing was supposed to end at nine o'clock, but the line of people went out of the Church and around the corner as that time approached. It looked like it was going to last a few more hours. I felt obligated to keep my plans with Matt, so I mentioned the situation to my uncle. He insisted that I leave to visit Matt and wouldn't hear another word about it. It made me feel bad to leave my family and the viewing, but I did.

GOD IS TALKING

The drive home remains vividly burned into my memory. I felt so utterly alone in the world. I don't think I will ever be able to fully express in words the emptiness I felt inside. I was utterly drained emotionally, mentally, and physically from everything I had been dealing with all week and the lack of sleep from the night before.

I called Matt the moment I got home. His Dad answered the phone. This is how our conversation went.
MATT'S DAD: Hello.
ME: Hello. Is Matt there?
MATT'S DAD: No, he is out with his girlfriend.
ME: Oh really? Are you sure?
MATT'S DAD: Yes.
ME: Could you have him call Sean when he gets home?
MATT'S DAD: Sure. Is this Sean from up the street?
ME: Yes.
MATT'S DAD: Okay, I'll have him call you.
ME: Thanks.
MATT'S DAD: Okay bye.
ME: Bye.

I figured Matt was out with his girlfriend to pass the time until I got home. I expected him to call me at any moment. I decided to turn on the TV to pass the time. The moment I sat down on the couch I realized how utterly exhausted I was. I turned the TV back off, placed the phone next to me, and put my head down. Within seconds I was sound asleep. Little did I know that something *big* was about to happen.

About ten minutes later, I woke up as if I had slept for ten hours. I thought it was strange how alert and full of energy I felt. Since I didn't know what to do with myself, I turned the TV back on.

One of Kim's favorite shows was on. I decided to watch it so that we could talk about it when I saw her the following evening. Much to my surprise, this particular episode was about a boy who had the stigmata. The stigmata are the wounds of the crucified Christ, "supernaturally" given to a normal human person. This causes them to bleed out of their hands and feet like Jesus did when He hung on the cross. One famous person that had the stigmata was St. Pio from Italy. I was surprised that a secular TV show would have an episode about something religious and spiritual like the stigmata. I watched the show with great interest because the stigmata had always fascinated me.

In the show, an evil person who had sold his soul to the devil was trying to kill the boy who had the stigmata. The main female character was chosen by God to protect the boy from the evil one.

As the show was coming to an end, I started wondering if I should try calling Matt again or maybe just take a ride down to his house to see if he was home. Maybe he was waiting for me in the band room out in his barn. Maybe he just forgot.

While I was thinking about what I should do, the character that was chosen to protect the boy with the stigmata went into a confessional and started talking to a priest. After a short time, the priest interrupted her and asked, "Are you here to make a confession or what, because you are not confessing any sins?" Without consciously realizing it, all of my attention went onto the TV screen almost as if a magnet was drawing me. I was fixated on what she was about to say. Time almost seemed to stop. Then she turned and seemed to look right at me, and said, "No. I guess I am here because… **God is talking, but no one is listening**."

BAMMMM! The moment those words reached my ears I felt like a bolt of lightning physically struck me in the heart! It didn't come from the TV show but from GOD! I was instantaneously aware of the sins I had been committing with my fiancé. I completely *knew* and understood within my soul that God was saying to me, "**IF YOU DO NOT CHANGE, YOU ARE GOING TO HELL.**" There was nowhere to run and nowhere to hide. The truth was clear, and it made me realize that I had been lying to myself and ignoring God. I had mentally convinced myself that it was okay for me to be having sex with Kim because I was planning to marry her. *I had rationalized my sins away so that I could live the way I wanted to live, but that didn't make it right in God's eyes.* God's commandments are not bendable. We can't make exceptions for ourselves whenever we want to. We either do what is right or we pay the price. For me, that meant I had to change, or I would end up in hell.

That night was very intense for me. I lay awake in bed for hours thinking about God, what He said, and what I was going to do. It was the most I had ever thought about God in one sitting. I really wanted to do the right thing. I didn't want to go to hell. I was afraid of spending all eternity suffering.

Before God gave me that message, I was hoping that sex would save my relationship with Kim. Now I had to make sure we didn't do it again until we were truly married or else I would end up in hell. I was very worried because I knew I didn't have the strength to say no to her. I also didn't think she would be very receptive to the idea of having to stop. This weighed heavily on my mind. My worries began to materialize in the words of my prayers.

Normally, I would just say some formalized prayers *about* God, but on this occasion I actually started talking *to* Him saying, "God, I don't want to go to hell. I want to do the right thing, but I know I don't have the strength." This was the only thing I could think to say, so I said it over and over for two whole hours without stopping.

COMFORTED

The next morning was pure white. It had been snowing for a long time, and it continued to come down hard. I began to think we might not make it to the funeral because the roads were so bad. We all piled into my dad's car and headed to the Church. It was a scary ride. The car seemed out of control most of the time. At one point, we even slid off the road into a ditch on the side of a big hill. My brother and I had to get out and push the car back onto the road, which was difficult to do in a suit and dress shoes. It took a long time to get to the Church, but we fortunately made it in time.

In order for you to understand something extremely significant that happened to me during the funeral Mass, I need to tell you about a secret that began when I was in eighth grade. Just before a religion test, our teacher reminded us that we had to have two quotes memorized from the bulletin board in the back of the classroom. Somehow I had completely missed that assignment. She told us we had two minutes to go back and look over the quotes before she handed out the test. I ran to the back of the room, picked out the two shortest quotes, and started cramming them into my brain. Miraculously, I remembered them both for the test. To this day, I still remember one of them. It goes like this, "The Lord is my shepherd. There is nothing I shall want." I liked this little quote so much that I adopted it as my secret little prayer between me and God. I added it to the list of prayers I said every night before falling asleep. I totally thought that I was the only person on earth who used this little quote as a prayer. With that in mind, I will tell you about the profound experience I had during the funeral Mass.

When it came time for the Responsorial Psalm, I heard the cantor sing my special little prayer. "The Lord is my shepherd. There is nothing I shall want." I quickly looked in the worship booklet I received before the service. When I reached the page with the Responsorial Psalm, I was amazed that it was right there in black and white. This was the first time I had seen or heard it in seven years. I never knew that I was praying a line from Psalm 23 all that time. When I heard the woman sing this Psalm, I had a profound spiritual experience of God inside of me. It felt like He was saying to me, "I am here with you. I put this in the ceremony for you. I have not left you Sean." This helped me so much! It still gives me the chills when I think about it. Before I heard that Psalm and felt God with me, I thought He hated me because of the sins I had committed. I thought He wanted me to go to hell. Having this happen uplifted my spirit and gave me strength and reassurance that God was still my friend.

After the Mass ended, we proceeded to the cemetery. It had stopped snowing, but the ground was covered with about six inches of snow. The cloud cover was extremely dense and expanded as far as my eyes could see in every direction. It was the kind of cloud cover that could last for days. Even though it was midday, the density of the clouds prevented the sunlight from coming through, which made it seem like nightfall. A miracle happened as we walked back to our cars from the gravesite. The dense cloud cover broke in one small area above the cemetery and rays of sunlight shone directly on the cemetery and nowhere else. They were mystical looking rays that came through the clouds in clear individual streams of light. The whole event lasted about five minutes. When it happened, I had a deep inner feeling that my cousin was in heaven, which was peacefully reassuring.

THE FINAL BLOW

The exams were finished. The viewing and funeral were now over. The last thing I had to deal with was the situation with Kim. My stomach would twist in knots every time I thought about her. I tried to keep myself preoccupied all day in order to pass the time. Five o'clock finally arrived! I sat by the phone anxiously anticipating Kim's call. My car keys were in my hand, so that I could jump in my car and drive over to see her the second we got off the phone. Time went by. I waited… and waited… and waited. Five thirty came and went. Six o'clock came and went. It turned six-twenty and she still had not called. The whole situation became more and more unbearable with each passing minute. I decided to give her until six-thirty. If I had not heard from her by then, I would try calling her. The clock struck six-thirty, and I quickly dialed.

Kim answered the phone. It was so nice to hear her soft voice. Within a minute of answering the phone, she said, "My mom just walked in the door, and I haven't had the chance to talk to her yet. Let me go talk to her, and I will call you back in a little bit." To me, a little bit meant fifteen minutes. I figured I could handle waiting a little longer even though I desperately wanted to see her. All I wanted was to be with her. I wanted the chance to look her in the eyes so that she would remember our love. I believed everything would be okay if we just had a chance to be together.

While I was waiting for Kim's call, my older brother was making plans to go to his friend's apartment to watch a heavyweight-boxing match on television. He invited me along. I told him I had plans, but wasn't sure what was happening with them yet. He told me to find out as soon as possible and let him know.

The situation with Kim was breaking my heart. Forty minutes passed, and she still had not called back. Filled with anxiety, I decided to call again. Her mom answered and told me Kim had gone babysitting. Although I was total a mess inside, I calmly and politely responded, "Really, we had plans to get together. May I please have the number where she is babysitting, so I can find out what is going on?" She said, "I don't know the number. I'll ask her brother if he knows. If he does, I will have him call you with it." Her statement troubled me. I believed she knew the number, but didn't want to tell me. I waited for about ten minutes for her brother to call, but he never did.

I called my friend Steve, the guy who brought Kim over to my house the summer before. It shocked me to find out that he was on the other line with her. When he told me that *she had called him*, I felt like I was punched in the gut! It made me feel so ill that I thought I was going to throw up. I furiously questioned in my mind, "WHAT IS SHE DOING CALLING HIM AND NOT EVEN CALLING ME? WHAT THE HECK IS GOING ON?" I asked him to have her call me. He relayed the message to her and then ended their conversation. Steve and I continued talking. Things were not sounding good. He wouldn't tell me what was going on. He said he promised Kim he wouldn't tell me anything. I desperately replied, "Come on! Tell me what's going on!" I begged him to tell me, but he wouldn't. "Come on man! PLEASE! TELL ME WHAT IS GOING ON!" I persisted until he finally started to crack. Just as he was about to give me some details, my other line beeped. It was Kim, so I immediately got off the phone with Steve in order to talk with her.

Although I was very upset, I managed to calmly and softly ask her,
ME: Why didn't you call me back?
KIM: I had to go babysitting. I needed the money.
ME: You could have told me. I would have understood. I've waited all this time to see you. I could wait one more day.
(*She didn't say anything.*)
ME: What are you doing tomorrow?
KIM: I have plans with my family.
(*Maintaining a very calm tone of voice, yet feeling desperate inside, I responded,*)
ME: Well... when am I going to see you?
KIM: I don't know.
(*This hurt me to hear. It sounded like she didn't even care about me. With a somewhat pleading voice, I asked,*)
ME: What do you mean you don't know? Don't you even want to see me?
(*She remained quiet. I didn't know what to do. My adrenaline started to rise. She wasn't putting any effort into our relationship.*

I thought that maybe I could say something to make her want to try harder.)
ME: Maybe we should break up.
(My hope was that she would say, "No" and want to make things work. Instead, she didn't say anything. I repeated myself hoping to get some kind of response from her.)
ME: Maybe we should break up.
(After a slight pause, she said,)
KIM: Yeah, I think that would be best.
(I anxiously responded,)
ME: No! We can work things out!
(She coldly responded,)
KIM: No... I don't think so.

I pleaded with Kim to stay with me, but she refused. I was helplessly trying to hold on, but there was nothing I could do. She broke up with me but agreed to exchange Christmas gifts. The next thing I knew our conversation ended.

I frantically called Steve back. After telling him what happened, I begged him to tell me what was going on. Reluctantly, he began to tell me what she told him. She had been spending a lot of time with her old boyfriend behind my back. He was the one who answered the phone the night I called her dorm room. Her sister never did go visit her that weekend. She had also made plans to spend New Year's Eve with him before we even broke up. This made my pain even worse because we made plans back in November to spend New Year's Eve together. Being cheated on, deceived, lied to, and dumped by my fiancé for another guy was the final and crushing blow to my agonizing week. I felt like I had been given more than I could handle. I was utterly destroyed inside.

NO ESCAPING IT

That night, I went out with my brother to watch the boxing match at his friend's apartment. I was in so much internal and emotional pain that I didn't even want to speak. I tried so hard to hide everything I was going through. Everyone was drinking, and I joined them. I wanted to drink until I couldn't think! I was hoping that the alcohol would take some of the pain away, but it didn't. The emotional pain persisted no matter how much I drank. It was a relentless pain that gnawed at every aspect of my existence.

Around one o'clock in the morning, my brother yelled, "HEY EVERYONE, SEANY'S 21!" I had recently turned 21 and it was my first time being around my brother and his friends since my birthday. They asked if I had gone to the casinos in New Jersey yet. I said, "No." They began a mild yelling chant that increased in volume as time went on. "ROAD TRIP! ROAD TRIP! ROAD TRIP! WE'RE TAKING SEANY TO THE CASINOS! WE'RE TAKING SEANY TO THE CASINOS!" The next thing I knew I was in the back of a car for a two hour ride headed to the casinos in New Jersey.

I only remember bits and pieces of the night. I remember sitting at a blackjack table. My vision was extremely blurry because I was so drunk, which is not something I am proud of, nor do I condone such behavior.

Everyone at the blackjack table was getting irritated with me. Apparently, what you do affects all the other players. If you mess up, it makes it harder for them to win. I was losing hand after hand, and people were jumping up in anger and leaving the table. After a while, some guy sat down next to me. He saw how miserably I was doing and started telling me how to play my cards. This caused me to start winning. It was a good thing too because I was almost out of chips. He left after a few minutes, and I proceeded to lose all of my money. The rest of the night was a blur, and I found myself in my bed at my parent's house the next morning.

PART FOUR—I've Got To Change!

GOD PLEASE HELP ME!

Kim stopped by to exchange Christmas gifts during the week. She gave back my crucifix ring. I told her to keep it, but she wouldn't. I longed for things to work out. I almost couldn't handle seeing her. The thought of losing her was crushing me. I wanted to hold her and kiss her, but I couldn't. I wished she would change her mind after seeing me, but she didn't.

The pain that I was living with was far worse than anything I had ever experienced. It was even worse than what I experienced from the breakup of my sinful relationship with Nancy at the end of high school. I would rather have gone through a hundred car accidents and a thousand surgeries than have to deal with the pain I was feeling inside. At least with physical pain you can take some kind of pain killer. You can't do that with emotional pain. There is no escaping it.

The only way I could temporarily avoid the suffering was to sleep. Three days passed, and I slept as much as my body would let me. I woke in the morning on the third day and begged, "Please, please fall back to sleep so that I don't have to think!" The more I thought, the more pain I felt. The more pain I felt, the more I thought about it. It was an unstoppable, self-destructive cycle. My misery intensified until it became unbearable! Without even realizing what I was doing, I cried out at the top of my lungs, "GOD, PLEASE HELP ME!" In that instant, I literally felt a heavy blanket of peace come down upon me. It went right through me and touched every part of my entire being, both inside and out. It took away *every* bit of pain I had inside.

The pain was replaced with a feeling of deep peace and incredible joy. I even started laughing. *It was amazing*! I couldn't believe what was happening to me. It surprised me so much that I wasn't even able to speak a clear sentence at first. With a huge smile on my face, I babbled, "You, ah, but, You just, I mean, You, You just answered my prayer! You're not supposed to do that. I thought all prayers were in vain! I thought I was down here doing my thing; You were up there doing Your thing, and some day I would die and come up there to meet You... but You... You... You just answered my prayer!"

I knew that I was experiencing God inside my soul in an utterly profound way. The feeling of His presence was by far the greatest experience of my life! The next thing I knew I was sitting up in bed excitedly yet seriously repeating over and over, "That's it! **I've got to change! I've got to change! I've got to change!**" I jumped out of bed and ran around my room yelling, "I've got to change! I've got to change! I've got to change!" I continued to have a massive smile on my face because of the joy I was experiencing.

As I stopped running, I thought, "God is real, and I have been living the wrong way!" I had to stop sinning and start living the way God expected me to. I knew that I had to make some kind of commitment to Him, or I would just slip back into my sinful ways as I had done in the past. I wouldn't have to deal with the issue of sex right away because my relationship with Kim was surely over. I had no intention of getting involved with anyone else for a long time. I needed to make a commitment to God about something that I could tangibly change right away.

The commitment that I needed to make came very clearly into my mind. It was obvious. My knees were shaking because of what I was about to say, but I knew I needed to say it. I was about to *vow* to God that I would *never* miss Sunday Mass ever again. Making this *vow* was very frightening. I thought to myself, "What if I do miss Mass? Then what am I going to do? I have missed it so many times in the past few years. Who is to say I won't do it again?" With extreme nervousness, I said out loud, "GOD, I *VOW* TO YOU THAT I WILL *NEVER* MISS MASS AGAIN!"

TIME TO LIVE IT

I went to my local Church on the following Sunday. This is where I went to elementary school, and where my parents took me to Church every single Sunday since before I can remember. I was in a very familiar place doing very familiar things, only this time I behaved differently. I picked up the songbook and made an effort to pay attention. I said to myself, "Well, since I am going to be here anyway, I might as well give it a hundred percent effort."

My old routine at Mass was to get there and then daydream until Mass was over. I started doing this around the age of twelve. In my Catholic school, certain students mocked you if you looked like you cared about Church or God. This left you with only a few basic options at Mass. One option was to look disinterested and tough. Another option was to respond very loudly and sarcastically, so that you appeared to be making fun of Mass. The last option was to stay silent and look like you hated being there.

Those days were over. I tried as hard as I could on this particular Sunday. Even though I tried earnestly, my singing volume was barely above a whisper. I was still deathly afraid of what other people would think of me, but the simple fact that I tried to participate made a huge difference. In addition to responding verbally to the prayers, I hung on every word that was said as if it was going to be the last word I would ever hear.

Through participating and listening intently, I could actually hear God speaking to me as we prayed. He spoke to me through the same prayers that we said *every single week* at Mass. They were no longer just words. They now brought life to me. Going to Church quickly became the most enjoyable element of my week. It gave me more happiness than any other activity. I never expected that to happen. All it took was a one hundred percent effort on my part.

It was easy to keep my *vow* of not missing Mass while I was at home for Christmas break. We lived five minutes away from my Church. I was worried about what I was going to do when I went back to school. I was unable to find a Church at school the last time I tried. What was going to make this time any different? My concerns were alleviated while I was clearing off the desk in my bedroom. Unexpectedly, I found an old letter that I had received from the Penn State Catholic Community before the school year began. I had assumed that they were just asking for money, so I had never opened it. The moment I found it sitting on my desk I was interested to see what was inside, so I tore it open. It contained a letter and a little card listing all the times and locations that Catholic Mass services were held on the school campus.

I said to myself, "No wonder I couldn't find a Church. The Mass services are held in classroom buildings." (This was before they built a new spiritual center on campus.) It seemed like God was giving me all the things I needed to keep my *vow* to Him. This made me very happy. I desperately wanted to pay God back for all the good He had done for me. I wanted to make up for all the ways I had sinned in the past. All I could think was, "GOD, I AM GOING TO PAY YOU BACK!"

Before God touched my life and gave me true happiness, I wanted to be a good person for my own sake. I said my prayers and went to Church because they were on the list of things I believed I needed to do in order to be a good person. The difference now was that I knew God and tasted how amazing He is. I now wanted to be a good person for His sake. I wanted to go to Church out of love and respect for Him, not just to fulfill an obligation. This may not sound like much on paper, but it was a major difference for me.

Just as God provided for me in this situation, He had also provided for me throughout my whole life. He had given me a good family, a good Catholic education, and a roof over my head. We always had food to eat. So many people had nothing compared to me. So much had been given to me, and I had taken it all for granted. I didn't want to do that anymore.

Although my life was changing, and spending time with God in Church made me very happy, the pain of losing Kim sometimes resurfaced. When this happened, I would put my fists together, one on top of the other, and hold them right in front of my heart. I would then close my eyes and imagine God's light shining out from the center of my heart as I prayed, "The Lord is my Shepherd, there is *nothing* I shall want!" Later I added to this prayer saying, "The Lord is the center of my life!" This helped me get through my times of trial. It helped me keep my focus on God and what He had done for me.

WHAT HAPPENED TO MATT?

I eventually talked to Matt while I was still at home for Christmas break. I asked him where he went with his girlfriend the Friday night of my cousin's viewing. With a confused look on his face, he asked, "What are you talking about?" I responded, "I called around nine, and your dad told me you were out with your girlfriend." His eyes opened wide with surprise as he replied, "That is really weird! I was home the whole night. I was upstairs in my bedroom when you called. I heard the phone ring and sat still listening and waiting for someone to tell me I had a phone call. I didn't hear anything, so I went downstairs to see if it was you. My dad was watching TV when I walked into the family room. I asked him if the phone call was for me. He said, 'No.' I asked, 'It wasn't Sean?' He said, 'No, it wasn't for you.' I even asked him again, 'You're sure it wasn't Sean?' He didn't respond because he was so engulfed with his TV show. After I stood there for a minute, I shrugged my shoulders and went back upstairs. I figured you had a lot to deal with, so I didn't want to call and bother you."

I was shocked by what Matt told me. As I thought about it later, I came to believe that God's hand was involved with the whole situation. If Matt had taken my call, I would have gone to his house to play the guitar that night. I never would have watched that TV show and received the message from God. Neither would I have spent hours praying to God regarding my life and my need to change.

THE MORE YOU GIVE, THE MORE YOU RECEIVE

When I attended Church, I constantly reminded myself that I was there to give God my best effort. This motivated me to overcome my insecurities and fears about singing and responding during Mass. I had to force myself with all my might to sing. At first, I needed people around me to sing louder than me so that I could sing under them without being noticed. As my confidence grew, so did my volume in responding. The more I sang and participated, the more I heard God speak to me.

When I returned to school after Christmas break, I started to attend Mass every Sunday as I had vowed to God. I always sat in the back of the congregation. No one had been participating at all back there until I came along. The more I made myself sing and participate, the more I could hear other people around me start to sing and participate. I could hear them whispering under me just as I had done when I started. They became louder and louder each week as their confidence grew. My efforts to contribute at Mass made a major difference. The whole area around me began to change. An obvious energy came from us as we prayed, and I could actually feel God's presence. I had no choice but to smile. I couldn't help it.

I believed that I was finally giving God what He deserved: my whole heart, mind, soul, and strength! I wished more people would make an effort at Mass so that they, and everyone else around them, could feel the happiness that it brings. I have heard it said, "It is through giving that we receive." I found this to be true when it came to giving of myself at Mass. If we make an effort, we are blessed.

Every person at the Church has an important role to play. The more we all give, the happier we all will be by the time we walk out of Church. If we do not give, we do not experience God, and we leave Church without feeling any better or more alive than when we went in. We end up cheating ourselves and everyone around us, which is a dreadful shame.

SPONSOR SOMEONE

Before I go any further, I want to tell you about the very first Mass I attended on campus at Penn State. I was sitting in the back of the congregation with a huge smile on my face. The priest got up at the end of Mass and made an announcement before giving the final blessing. He said with a strong intensity, "There are forty students who are going through the RCIA program. RCIA means 'Rite of Christian Initiation for Adults.' This program enables adults to be baptized, receive their first Holy Communion, and Confirmation. I'm embarrassed to say that we do not have enough people to sponsor them. There are ten thousand registered Catholic students on this campus. We need some of you to step forward and sponsor our candidates and catechumens. We are also in need of more Extraordinary Ministers of the Eucharist to help with the distribution of Holy Communion at Mass. We need Lectors to do the readings, and Hospitality Ministers to greet people at the doors and set up for Mass."

The things he talked about provided me with an opportunity to give back. As I walked home from Mass, I thought to myself, "I would like to be a sponsor... but... I just don't have the time. I am not a good reader, so I can't do the Lector thing. I wouldn't like being a Hospitality Minister and have to greet everyone at the door. I guess I could do the Extraordinary Minister of the Eucharist thing. All you really need to do is stand up there and hand out Communion. That doesn't sound too hard. I am going to be at Church anyway. Yeah, I'll do that."

A training session for people who wanted to become an Extraordinary Minister of the Eucharist was being held the following Saturday. I planned to attend. As Friday rolled around, so did my "friends." They pressured me into going out to a party with them. I was still very afraid and quiet about my faith outside of Church, so I didn't put up much resistance. As a result of my late night, I slept in and missed the training workshop. I failed in my attempt to give back to God. This made me feel awful, and I regretted going out the night before.

I found my social life to be very difficult. I didn't want to go partying or drinking anymore, but my friends were fixated on it. I wanted some new friends who were more into religion but had not found any yet.

The next day I went to Sunday Mass. There was an announcement near the end that presented me with a welcome surprise. I had the date wrong for the Extraordinary Ministers of the Eucharist training session. The actual meeting was not until the following weekend. I firmly resolved right then and there that I would *not* miss the training session and that I would *not* go out the night before. Friday came, and I avoided everyone. I can't remember exactly what I did, but I think I went to the library to study until it got pretty late.

The training session started in late morning, and I was there. The priest stopped to introduce himself to me before the meeting officially began. I told him I was at the Mass when he mentioned the need for RCIA sponsors and other volunteers. I was about to tell him that I wished I could help out with RCIA, but I didn't have the time. My main reason was because I had just become the president of the Penn State Archery Club, which used up all my extra time. Before I had a chance to say anything, he jumped in and energetically said, "Oh good! RCIA meetings are every Thursday night from seven to nine and every Sunday morning at the eleven-thirty Mass. The candidates who have not received their first Holy Communion and the catechumens leave after the readings to discuss them together. You can go to another Mass to receive Communion. You will also need to stay here for Easter because that is when they will receive their Sacraments and become fully initiated into the Catholic Church. So you can do it!"

His last sentence would normally be worded as a question, but he worded it like an excited statement. I felt like I had just been hit in the face with a series of lefts and rights, which left me feeling dazed and confused. I always had a hard time saying no to someone when they put me on the spot like that. I hesitantly said, "Uuuuummm… sure." As he walked away, he excitedly said, "Good! I will see you this Thursday night." Feeling puzzled and overcome, I thought to myself, "What in the world just happened? Well… it looks like I am going to be a sponsor…" This meant I would have to adjust my archery schedule.

The Eucharistic training session went well, and I immediately got involved with distributing Holy Communion at Mass. I really enjoyed being an Extraordinary Minister of the Eucharist. It felt good to do something for God and give something back in the form of service. Little by little, I moved up each week from the back of the congregation toward the front. After a few weeks, I found myself near the front row. I admired the people who were already up in the front and were not afraid to sing out and pray openly. I remember saying to myself, "I want to be like them." They had been serious about their relationship with God for a long time and didn't care what other people thought of them. After observing their example, it sometimes bothered me that I had wasted so much of my life being away from God. There was so much to make up for and so little time to do it.

Much to my surprise, becoming an RCIA sponsor was the best thing I ever could have done. Every meeting enriched me so much. I loved it. When I went to Catholic school, I spent most of my time disinterested and daydreaming. When I graduated from high school, I actually said, "Well at least I never have to study religion again." Now that I was actively seeking God I absorbed every teaching they shared. The Catholic Faith that I was forced to learn while I was growing up was now being presented to me again only this time I *wanted it*! I was like a dry sponge soaking up water. I thought I was there to be a sponsor and help someone else. I thought I was going there to give back to God and do something good. I did not anticipate feeling so enriched and fulfilled from every meeting. They always left me feeling nourished and alive. It was awesome!

One session in particular stands out in my mind. We were in the Meditation Chapel for a small group discussion. Questions were pounding in my mind. All I could think was, "Why me? Why me God? Why did You choose me? Look at all the students on this campus. Why did you choose me? Why not one of them?" I just couldn't understand why God had done so much for me. It seemed like all of the other students were throwing their lives away with drinking and partying. God pulled me out of that mess and made me truly happy, happy to be with Him! I used to lie to myself and everyone else, pretending that I was having fun at parties, but I never really did. While all the noise and commotion was going on at parties, I sometimes had a deep down feeling of aloneness. All the things that were supposed to make me happy never really did. Instead, I was finding true happiness in God and in going to Church.

TRYING TO CHANGE

Taking a good look at my life, I picked out the main things that I needed to **change** and worked very hard at them! The drinking and partying had to stop! Even though I really wanted to totally stop doing wrong all at once, I couldn't. Getting rid of the drinking and partying was harder than I imagined it would be. What made it so difficult was the pressure I received from the people around me. At first I found myself making compromises to keep everyone happy, but the compromises turned into terrible backslides. Every time I made a big mistake, I'd get very angry with myself. I was determined not to fail again. I kept trying to do what was right.

The drinking and partying difficulty came mainly on the weekends. There was something else I needed to change that happened throughout the day all week long. I still used foul language excessively. Every other word that came out of my mouth was a cuss word. It was difficult to correct because I said so many bad words without even realizing it. Little by little I became more aware of them and tried to hold them back.

The weekend after I started my major effort to quit cussing, I visited an old friend at a distant college. He also had a very foul mouth. He had been trying to quit using the "F" word because the girl he liked wouldn't tolerate it. They came up with a rule together. If he ever said the "F" word in front of her, he had to get down on the ground and do a push-up. I liked the idea and adopted it for myself. This really helped me become aware of my language fast. The embarrassment of having to get down on the ground and do a push-up was all I needed to make me sharply aware of my use of that word. After weeks of hard work, I finally kicked my bad language habit. It was a long, hard-fought battle, but I came out on top!

An interesting thing happened to me after I had overcome my foul language problem. I was home visiting my family for the weekend. Someone was watching an R-rated movie in the family room, and I sat down to watch it with them. It seemed like every other word in the movie was the "F" word. This really bothered me because I had become so sensitive to the use of that word. When I first started watching the movie, I almost wanted to get down on the ground and start doing pushups just from hearing it. As the movie progressed, and the more I heard the "F" word, the less it bothered me. Without fully realizing it, I was becoming desensitized. I walked into our kitchen after the movie ended. Without thinking about it, the "F" word came out of my mouth while I was standing there looking for something to eat.

I struggled intensely with my language problem for days after seeing that movie. This really upset me. I had spent so much time and effort overcoming this problem, and it came back after watching just one R-rated movie. This experience taught me a valuable lesson. I learned how much movies, music, and television can strongly influence me without me even being aware of it. This made me realize that I would have to give up certain R-rated movies, television shows, and music that I liked because they were a *negative influence*. It was more important for me to be pure and stay pure than it was for me to expose myself to those negative influences. I knew I could live without them, and so I chose to remove them from my life.

TIME TO CONFESS

The priest told us at one of the RCIA meetings that we should all go to Confession before Easter. He also said that we should plan to go to Confession at least once a year. I quietly disagreed with his statement. I thought that I could confess my sins right to God, and didn't need to go to a priest. I didn't believe we had to tell someone else our sins in order to be forgiven by God. I believed God heard me and forgave me when I asked Him for forgiveness. Confession never seemed to do anything for me anyway.

Back in elementary and high school, when they made us go to Confession, I always gave the priest the same list of sins. The list sounded like this: "I cheated on a test, lied to my mom, and fought with my brother." When I told the priest these sins, he told me to say some prayers and that was it. It was the same thing every time. Still, I must admit that another reason I didn't want to go to Confession was that I hadn't gone in years!

Even though I tried to convince myself that I didn't need to go to Confession, the priest's words ate away at my mind. His statement bothered me so much, that the only thing I could do to ease my mind was to actually go to Confession. I didn't realize it at the time, but it was the Holy Spirit working with my conscience to help me become properly reconciled with God. I wasn't used to listening to my conscience. I was used to distracting myself or convincing myself to just forget personal issues that I didn't want anyone to know about.

I went to Confession the next day. It was in a small Catholic Chapel on campus next to the location they were building the new spiritual center. The line for Confession was long. A somewhat awkward silence filled the small narrow hallway where we all were standing. While I waited, I resolved to actually admit the major sin that I had kept hidden from everyone. My plan was to go in, kneel behind the screen, tell the priest I had sex with Kim, and then hightail it out of there.

The tension began to build in my neck as my turn approached. I was extremely nervous but tried to not think about what I was about to do. If I had allowed myself to think about saying my hidden sin out loud to someone, I would have been overcome with fear and anxiety. I probably would not have been able to confess it.

Finally, it was my turn. I took a deep breath, walked into the Chapel, closed the door, and turned around expecting to see a big screen for me to kneel behind. I was shocked to see the priest from the RCIA program sitting there looking at me. I hysterically thought, "OH NO! HE SEES ME!" I wanted to turn and run back out the door, but that would have been even more awkward than staying and going through with it. Having to tell my sin to him face to face made it ten thousand times harder to do! I thought that every time he looked at me he would see my sins written across my forehead. I thought my reputation in his eyes would be forever ruined. As I sat down in front of him, I could feel nervous tension throughout my body. Struggling to overcome my fears, I began to make the Sign of the Cross. I couldn't even look him in the eyes; I just continued with the ritual of Confession. I told him that it had been at least three years since my last Confession. He made a sound to acknowledge my statement. I then confessed what I believed to be my worst sin ever. It was gut-wrenchingly difficult for me to do, but I admitted that I had had sex with Kim. The priest stunned me by asking two questions as soon as I told him this. The first was, "Is this something that happened often?" The second question was, "Is she the only one you did this with?" I was so startled that I reacted nervously. I responded without even thinking. I blurted out, "She was the only one, and not often." It was so hard for me to even admit I had had sex outside of marriage, that being put on the spot with his questions was too much for me to handle.

He then asked me if there was anything else I wanted to confess. I told him I had missed Sunday Mass on many occasions. After I finished confessing my sins, he asked me to make an Act of Contrition. It had been so long since I had recited that prayer that I didn't fully remember it. He had to help me get through it by having me repeat after him, "Oh my God. I am heartily sorry for having offended You. And I detest all of my sins because of Your just punishments, but most of all because they offend You my God, who are all good and deserving of all my love. I firmly resolve, with the help of Your grace, to sin no more, and to avoid the near occasions of sin. Amen."

Even though I was not able to answer the priest's questions honestly, God seriously honored my heartfelt effort to confess this sin for the first time. *It was amazing*! I felt like the weight of the world was lifted off my shoulders! It had been there for so long that I didn't even realize I was carrying it. The awful burden was replaced with a tingly, weightless, exhilarating feeling. I felt so free! As I was leaving the confessional, I actually had to look down at my feet to make sure they were still touching the ground. I felt like I was floating on air. I wouldn't have been able to wipe the smile off my face even if I wanted to. I couldn't believe what happened inside of me just from going to Confession!

Instead of giving me prayers to say for my penance, the priest told me to call Kim and ask her how she was doing. This was very hard for me to do. I didn't want to call her. I didn't want her to think I was still after her, or that I was still in love with her. When I got to my apartment, I went into my bedroom and closed the door. My hands were trembling and my gut was twisting as I walked over to the phone. I began to sweat and feel sick in my stomach as I dialed. Kim answered the phone with a soft, pleasant sounding voice. Still feeling anxious and nauseous, I asked her how she was doing. She said she was doing fine. We had an easy-going conversation for a few minutes before hanging up. After that phone call, I felt all the more ready to let go of our relationship and move on with my life. I felt good about myself for having confessed my sins and for fulfilling my difficult penance.

After that, I built up enough courage to go back to Confession. I admitted to the priest that I was not honest in my responses to his questions in my last Confession. After I corrected my answers to his questions, he commended me for my courage. He also said he was proud of me for having the strength to bring my sins before the Lord. With that, my slate was completely wiped clean, and I had a brand new start in life!

LENT

Lent came. For the first time in my life, I really wanted to observe the Lenten Fast. I decided to fast on bread and water for forty days. I wanted to give up drinking alcohol, and Lent was the perfect opportunity to do it. If my friends asked me to go out partying and drinking with them, I planned to just say, "No, I gave it up for Lent."

I started Lent with a lot of fervor. I ate only bread and water for a while. As time went by, fasting became a struggle. It left me feeling tired, weak, dizzy, and light-headed. After about two weeks, I began to make exceptions and ate more and more.

Half way through lent, a major dilemma came my way. My friend Brad was turning twenty-one. For an entire week, he bugged me with questions like, "Are you going bar-hopping with me on my birthday?" He wouldn't accept that I had given up drinking for Lent. He relentlessly pestered me with statements like, "Come on man! It's my twenty-first birthday! It only comes once! Come on! You gotta come out! You could just have one drink with me!" His constant pestering wore me out. I eventually agreed to go out, but I insisted that I would *not* drink. As soon as I said I would go, Brad carried on saying, "Come on! You can have just one! God understands! Come on! This will be the only time I will ever turn twenty-one! You gotta have a drink with me!" I said "No." This went on for days. After his torturous, relentless pestering, I began to break down until finally I agreed to have *one drink* with him on his birthday.

On the night of Brad's birthday, I walked to the first bar to meet with him and his fraternity brothers. I really fought with myself about it. I had done very well not drinking throughout Lent and didn't want to ruin it. When I got to the bar, Brad and his fraternity brothers appeared to have been drinking for a while. I didn't know anyone except Brad. Normally, everyone buys the birthday boy a drink. In this situation, Brad bought me a drink. He put it in my hand before I even had a chance to wish him happy birthday. He smiled as he handed it to me. It seemed like a deceptive smile, and I didn't feel right about the situation. It seemed like everyone was watching me. I wondered what they were thinking. Many pressuring thoughts fired through my mind, and I gave in. As I raised the glass to my mouth, I promised God that I would have only *one* drink. I told Him I would make it up to Him in some way. Maybe I would do an extra week of fasting or something really difficult.

I stood there sipping the beer, feeling like an outsider. Everyone was talking and laughing about fraternity things, which I knew nothing about. As I approached the bottom of the beer, I started planning my exit. I was trying to figure out what I could say to make it sound like I really needed to go. The next thing I knew Brad pulled the glass out of my hand and replaced it with a fresh, cold, full mug of beer. This created a major dilemma for me. I looked around. It seemed like everyone was laughing and having a good time. I wanted to have a good time too. I asked myself, "What about being a good example? What about stopping after one?" I found myself struggling with a part of me that didn't want to stop. Questions started to race through my mind like, "What is happening to me? Where did my desire to quit drinking go?"

It suddenly became easier to think of reasons why it was okay to have one more. "You already had one. Why not just enjoy yourself? It is only one night. It's his birthday. It's a day to celebrate." Brad stared at me as I stood there with the second glass of beer in my hand. The loud bar seemed to become quiet. The stained-glass light fixtures above us reflected various colors off the glass of beer as I slowly raised it to my lips. I felt a cold chill when it rushed down my throat. As I brought the glass back down, my vision came back into focus on Brad's face. His eyes glared with satisfaction. He grinned slightly, then turned around and walked back over to his fraternity brothers, leaving me there alone with the new beer. I forced myself to numb my guilty thoughts so that I didn't think about what I had just done. I didn't even realize that I was being led down a slippery slope.

We drank several more beers and hit several more bars before something tragic happened to me. We had to show our ID cards at the door to get into the next bar. I felt rushed and pressured to be quick. There was a long line of people standing behind me waiting to get in out of the cold, snowy weather. I quickly reached into my pocket for my driver's license. As I tried to pull my hand out, the cross bar of my crucifix ring got hung up on the top inside edge of my pocket. In my somewhat drunken state, I haphazardly pulled my hand with a stern jolt to get it out of my pocket. The crossbar of the crucifix ring dug sharply into my pinky finger and left a very painful mark as it ripped down and off of my pinky. It pulsated with pain, as I handed my ID card to the bouncer. While he took it, I frantically looked down. The floor was dark, dirty, and drenched with beer and melted snow. I nervously scanned the area in every direction as fast as I could. I did not see my special crucifix ring. The bouncer handed back my ID card. I had no choice but to move in so that others could come in behind me. The music was loud. The bar was very dark and crowded. I had to think fast. I diligently looked around as I moved out of the way, but I still didn't see my ring. I decided that my best option was to come back in the morning as soon as they opened. I figured I would be able to find it when the lights were on and the place was empty.

Early the next morning I called to find out the exact time they opened. I went there before any customers arrived. My heart sank the moment I walked in the door. The floor had been completely swept and mopped clean and dry. It was so clean that I knew there was no chance they would have missed my ring in the cleaning process. I went to the counter and asked a worker if anyone had found a ring while mopping the floor. The guy sounded very annoyed by my question and sharply responded, "No!" then turned back to what he was doing.

I just stood there for a moment in disbelief. That ring meant so much to me, and it was gone, gone forever! All those years I had looked forward to giving it to the girl I was going to marry were stripped away from me in one brief passing moment. As I walked home, I felt like it was God's way of punishing me for drinking and breaking my Lenten promise. I felt like I deserved it. I went to Confession for what I had done and started over. God forgave me, but the pain of losing my ring and what it meant to me didn't go away easily.

EASTER

All of the candidates and catechumens in the RCIA program were scheduled to receive their Sacraments at the Easter Vigil Mass. I wanted it to be a very special and powerful night for the girl I was sponsoring. I dressed in my best clothes for this occasion. It had been a long time since I wore my dress shoes. I didn't realize I had grown out of them until my feet started to hurt very badly a half-hour into the ceremony. The liturgy lasted for three hours.

Despite the pain in my feet, I remained focused and intense the entire time. I hoped that the more I put into the prayers and the service, the more the girl I was sponsoring would get out of it. I vividly remember the moment she was baptized. I placed my hand on her shoulder and prayed fervently for her whole life. I wanted the best for her. I wanted God to bless everything she did. I wanted her to be truly happy in life.

After the Easter Vigil Mass, one of the sponsors invited me to the nonalcoholic party her boyfriend was having. I didn't have anything else to do, so I went. It was an uncomfortable situation for me. I didn't know the guy who was hosting the party, and I didn't know any of his friends. I was intimidated by the situation and hoped that someone would talk to me. I ended up standing in the corner by myself. Several of the guys started playfully throwing chocolate candy at each other, which turned into a major fiasco. This just wasn't my scene, so I didn't stay long. It was my first Easter away from home, and I felt all alone. I had been begging God for some good Catholic Christian friends to share my faith with, but I still hadn't connected with any. For a long time, I felt like it was just me and God against the world.

NOW WHAT CAN I DO FOR GOD?

Being a sponsor was an incredibly life-giving and enriching experience for me, but it ended at the Easter Vigil Mass. This motivated me to look for more things to do for God. The more I did for God by getting involved with my Church, the happier I was becoming in life. I wanted to do things for Him every day, but the only thing that seemed available was daily Mass.

After wrestling with myself about it for a long time, I decided to try going to Mass on a Tuesday afternoon. I still remember my playful thoughts as I sat in the pew waiting for Mass to begin. "I can't believe I am here for daily Mass! Hello! Me... We're talking about me... Sean McVeigh... at daily Mass! What is the world coming to?" It seemed like I had changed so much in just a short period of time! Before my profound experience of God after Kim dumped me, God was a rare thought in my mind. Now He was becoming the ultimate focus of my life.

JESUS, IF THAT'S YOU, PROVE IT

Something utterly significant dawned on me after I began attending Mass every day. It happened during the words of Consecration at Mass. The words of Consecration are the words that Jesus said at the Last Supper after lifting a piece of bread, "Take and eat; this is My body," after taking a cup of wine He said, "Drink from it, all of you, for this is My blood of the covenant, which will be shed on behalf of many for the forgiveness of sins." (Matthew 26:26-28) As the priest said those words, I realized that the Catholic Church believes in Transubstantiation. This means that the bread actually becomes Jesus' body, and the wine actually becomes His blood. "WAIT A SECOND! THAT CAN'T BE RIGHT!" I exclaimed in my mind. I remembered back in the sixth grade thinking things like, "It looks like bread. It tastes like bread. It must be bread. It can't possibly be Jesus' actual body and blood." I concluded back then that the Protestants must be right about this issue. Several Protestant denominations believe in Consubstantiation, which means that Jesus is just spiritually present, and the bread and wine do not change into the actual body and blood of Jesus.

I found myself questioning the teaching of Transubstantiation in my mind. "How could the Catholic Church come up with such a belief from just a few lines of Scripture? I have heard these words my whole life. They just aren't enough for me to believe that the bread and wine literally became Jesus' flesh and blood." I started to pray about it.

"Lord, I just want You. All I want is You! I want You to lead me to the *truth*, so that I can grow as close to You as possible while I am here on earth. I want You to lead me to the right Church, so that I can follow the right teachings about You! There are a lot of other Churches out there. They all seem to study the Bible real hard. Maybe one of them has it right and the Catholic Church is wrong. Since I've been raised Catholic, and all I know is the Catholic Church, I will be Catholic for one week. For my part, I will do my best to actually believe what Catholics believe. I am asking You to prove to me *that it really is You in the Eucharist*! If You don't prove it to me, then I am leaving the Catholic Church, and I ask You to lead me to the right Church."

This was the prayer I was inspired to pray, and I said it with intense sincerity of heart. I believed God would honor my desire to get closer to Him by leading me to the right Church, so that I could learn the authentic truth about Him and His ways.

The next day was the first day of the one-week period. I didn't know if anything would happen to make me believe that the Eucharist was the true body and blood of Jesus, but I was curious to find out. I started the Mass relentlessly saying to Jesus, "I believe that You are truly present in the Eucharist!" After a while, I shortened it to, "I believe, I believe, I believe." As I was saying these words over and over in my mind, I knew within myself that I didn't believe. Despite my lack of faith, I kept saying it. I wanted to try being a Catholic for one week, which meant believing their teachings. I wanted to honor my side of my prayer intention, and I believed God would honor His.

When it came time for the words of Consecration, "This is My body..." my mind was flooded with intense thoughts of disbelief. To combat it, I vigorously repeated even harder in my mind, "I BELIEVE, I BELIEVE, I BELIEVE!" The doubting thoughts continued to *hammer* into the left side of my head. The sneering thoughts said, "NO YOU DON'T! YOU DON'T BELIEVE! Look at yourself! You are making a fool of yourself! You are brainwashing yourself!" These thoughts pounded at me so intensely that I physically felt stressed and began to perspire. Then a different set of thoughts entered my head from the other side. The other thoughts said, "If you are brainwashing yourself, then you are brainwashing yourself back to the truth." I felt mentally tortured, so I yelled inside my head, "SHUT UP! I BELIEVE, I BE-

LIEVE, I BELIEVE!" Beads of sweat trickled down my face and my back from this strenuous spiritual experience. After this happened, I began to worry that I might be turning schizophrenic or something.

Nothing happened at Mass on the first day that proved to me that Jesus is truly present in the Eucharist. I wanted an answer to my question, so I began to do some research. When I got home from Mass, I read all of the Gospel accounts of the Last Supper. I needed something more than just the words of Consecration to be able to believe that Jesus is truly present in the Eucharist.

The first Gospel account I read was Matthew 26:26-28. Nothing in that passage enabled me to believe. Reading Mark and Luke didn't help either. This caused me to say, "I needed *more*! There has to be something *more*!" I was surprised to find out that John didn't even depict Jesus turning the bread and wine into His body and blood at the Last Supper. Instead, John shows Jesus washing the feet of the Apostles in order to give them an example to follow.

The next day at Mass was a repeat of the first day. The argument in my head was violent and fierce. No matter how difficult it got, I kept repeating, "I believe, I believe, I believe!" I wanted to be faithful in my attempt to be a Catholic for one week. Let me tell you, it is harder to have the faith of a Catholic than you think!

Mass ended, and all I got out of it was a strained feeling and a sweat bath. Before I left to go home that day, I asked a very devout Catholic guy if there was anything else in the Bible on the Eucharist other than at the Last Supper. He quickly responded, "Yes, in John chapter six. I think it is somewhere around verse forty." It shocked me to hear that it was so early in the Gospel. I expected it to be near the end.

I quickly walked home, got out my Bible, and started to read the Gospel of John chapter six. I was on a quest, a quest for the truth! Before long, I came to the part that says:

> This is the bread that comes down from heaven that one may eat of it and not die. I am the living bread that came down from heaven; whoever eats this bread will live forever; and the

bread that I will give **IS MY FLESH** for the life of the world. (John 6:50-51)

As I read that last line, I felt something burst inside of me. I was immediately filled with the most intense and amazing feeling of *joy*! It literally felt like I floated up off the floor. At the same time, I was filled with an incredible, powerful gift of *faith*! I suddenly had absolute and total belief that the Eucharist really, truly, and absolutely *is* the body, blood, soul, and divinity of Jesus Christ, physically present in every Catholic Church throughout the world. I also knew I needed to receive Him in the Eucharist for my salvation. My feeling of faith in the miracle of the Eucharist was so potent, that I could easily tell it was not coming from me. It was coming from God Himself. I could hardly contain myself and the joy I was experiencing at that moment. I managed to read on with intense excitement:

> The Jews quarreled among themselves saying, 'How can this man give us *His flesh to eat?*' Jesus said to them, 'Amen, amen, I say to you, unless you *eat* the flesh of the Son of Man and drink His blood, you do not have life within you. Whoever *eats My flesh* and drinks My blood has eternal life, and I will raise him on the last day. **FOR MY FLESH IS TRUE FOOD, AND MY BLOOD IS TRUE DRINK**. Whoever *eats My flesh* and drinks My blood remains in Me and I in him. Just as the living Father sent Me and I have life because of the Father, so also the one who feeds on Me will have life because of Me. This is the bread that came down from heaven. Unlike your ancestors who ate and still died, whoever *eats* this bread will live forever.' (John 6:52-58)

As I read through those lines, I felt like I was becoming more and more alive with each passing word. My belief in this teaching grew stronger and stronger! I felt like excitedly running in circles around my little bedroom where I was standing. I started exuberantly yelling out loud, "IT'S TRUE! IT'S TRUE! IT REALLY IS JESUS! WOW! IT'S TRUE! HOW COME NO ONE EVER SHOWED ME THIS PASSAGE BEFORE? I'VE BEEN CATH-

OLIC MY WHOLE LIFE AND NO ONE EVER TOLD ME ABOUT THIS PASSAGE! I'VE GOT TO TELL THE WHOLE WORD ABOUT THIS! HOW COULD ANYONE NOT BELIEVE?" My mind continued to race with thoughts like, "That means that Catholics are right! I am in the right Church!" Inside my soul I felt like a little kid being handed a lollipop as a reward for my strenuous efforts!

God gave me yet another reward a few days later while I was home visiting my family for the weekend. They had recently gotten the Catholic television station known as EWTN. I had heard a lot about it but had never seen it. The show that was on when I tuned into EWTN was about documented, scientifically proven, Eucharistic miracles. Jesus has actually worked numerous miracles throughout history to prove to the world that He is truly present in the Eucharist: body, blood, soul, and divinity! I couldn't believe my eyes! The show mentioned several books that record these Eucharistic miracles. This totally amazed me. It reaffirmed my newly acquired *faith*. By the end of the show, I felt like a little kid being given yet another lollipop as a reward for my hard-fought spiritual battle to find the true Church!

SATURDAY NIGHT PRAYER GROUP

A few weeks had passed since I started going to Mass every day. I was high on life because of my newfound faith, my relationship with God, and my involvement with the Catholic Church! At the end of Sunday Mass, they announced that there would be a prayer group meeting the following Saturday night. I was very excited to hear this. I thought to myself, "Finally, I can do something for God on Saturday night and not have to make up excuses as to why I don't want to go out drinking!"

Throughout the week, I thought about the Saturday night prayer group meeting. My anticipation was building with each passing day. I expected to go to the meeting, pray some "Our Fathers," and sing some familiar Church songs. I hoped I would make some new friends after the meeting was over.

When I got to the meeting, I recognized a number of people from daily Mass and the RCIA program. The music minister stood up and said, "Okay everybody, let's stand and start by singing song number twenty three." Everyone jumped up and began swaying as the guitar started playing. They were clapping their hands and singing at the top of their lungs with their eyes closed. This startled me. I did not expect this at all. I was not used to this kind of behavior in Church. The old-school nuns that taught me in elementary school wouldn't even let us stand crooked in Church. Swaying and clapping were definitely out of the question.

I felt extremely uncomfortable, and gripped the song sheet with all my might. My knuckles turned bright white from the intensity of my grip. My posture was as stiff as a board. It only got worse when the song ended. People were chanting all kinds of weird things. It freaked me out in a major way! It put me over the edge when I saw one of the teachers from the RCIA program sitting Indian style on the floor with her eyes closed. She was rocking back and forth chanting in a long drawn out tone, "JESUS… JESUS… JESUS…" I wanted to turn and *run* out the door as fast as I could. Since I didn't want to be seen leaving, I stayed and tried to cope with the situation.

I was uncomfortable and tense the whole time. It was a two-hour meeting. I spent the first hour trying to calm down. I kept reminding myself that I was there for God, and I did my best to pray to Him in my own way.

Eventually they stopped singing and had everyone sit down. Two students got up and explained what was going on. They called it "Charismatic prayer," and said that people were using the "Gifts of the Holy Spirit." These gifts were "Tongues, Prophecy, and Healing." Praying in tongues meant letting the Holy Spirit pray through you in foreign languages, similar to what happened to the Apostles in the book of Acts. This explained all the strange things they were chanting between songs. Prophecy is when God gives a message to someone in the prayer group and that individual relays the message to everyone else. Healing is a gift from the Holy Spirit to cure physical, spiritual, and emotional wounds of the people who are present at the prayer meeting.

I had been a Catholic my whole life and never heard of these gifts. The Gifts of the Holy Spirit had been explained differently to me in the past. In my Confirmation class and in the RCIA program, they taught me that the Gifts of the Holy Spirit were, "Wisdom, Counsel, Understanding, Knowledge, Fortitude, Piety, and Fear of the Lord."

I pondered this topic years later to figure out what I perceived the difference to be. It seemed to me that the Charismatic Gifts of the Holy Spirit were manifestations that occur in prayer group settings. These gifts help people worship God, and they build up the body of believers. The gifts that I learned about in RCIA and Confirmation class had to do with special graces each one of us receives from the Holy Spirit through Baptism and Confirmation. These graces help us grow every day in our faith relationship with God and in service of others.

Halfway through the meeting one of the leaders got up and told everyone what God was doing in his life. This was called "giving a testimony," or "faith sharing." After both leaders gave their testimonies, they invited us to get up one at a time and give our own testimony. We didn't have to do it, so I chose *not* to.

Most of the testimonies were people talking about Jesus and the Holy Spirit. This helped me realize that I had always viewed God as the Father. Although I believed in Jesus and the Holy Spirit as part of the Trinity, I never really thought very much about them or prayed to them. I thought about why this was. One reason was because of the visit I received from God the Father during my first year of college. Another reason was because the prayers that we said at Mass seemed to be directed primarily at God the Father. I also realized I was afraid of the name of Jesus because of some of my influential high school classmates. They sternly made fun of people who talked about Jesus. Also, the Bible-thumping TV Evangelists who constantly used Jesus' name really turned me off. I did *not* want to be like them. For these reasons, I had developed a resistance to the name of Jesus without even realizing it.

After hearing the testimonies of the students, I wanted to get to know Jesus and the Holy Spirit better. I made a conscious choice to start praying more to Jesus and not just to the Father. I wanted to become comfortable praying in Jesus' name. In addition, I planned to think more about the Holy Spirit when I prayed. I decided to ask the Holy Spirit to guide and enlighten my prayers. Lastly, I wanted to become more aware of the workings of the Holy Spirit in my everyday life.

Near the end of the meeting I began to experience a deep peace. This was a delightful surprise! The feeling of peace soaked so deeply into me that I knew it was not something I could create on my own. It was coming from the Holy Spirit, and it was something that my soul desperately longed for on a daily basis.

I felt so good after the prayer group meeting that I immediately decided to come back the following month. Even though I planned to return, I still didn't know what to think about the crazy things that were going on with the Charismatic Gifts of the Holy Spirit. I doubted the validity of tongues. Some people sounded like they were just doing it to fit in. At the same time, I could not deny that some people sounded authentically spiritual when they prayed in tongues. Because of them, I remained open to the possibility that tongues could be real. I also didn't know what to make of the gift of prophecy. Would God really give us messages like that? I was undecided but planned to think about it more.

MAJOR DISAPPOINTMENT

After the meeting, I was invited to the party that everyone was going to. This was very exciting for me. I hoped that I would finally make some good Catholic friends. It made me happy to think that I would get to be with people who knew how to enjoy themselves without using alcohol. I wanted to live the right way, the way God intended us to live. I believed these people were already doing it.

I walked to the party filled with anticipation! My hopes were high! One of the guys I admired the most, because of his involvement with his faith, was standing outside the house as I approached. My heart sank a million miles into the earth when I saw him holding a beer and collecting money from the people who wanted to drink from the keg. My expectations were destroyed. They were doing the very same thing I wanted so badly to get away from. I stood there stunned and disappointed for a moment, then turned and walked home before anyone saw me.

As I walked home, I felt so sad and alone. A fire started welling up within me. I sternly thought to myself, "If no one else is going to be the example, then I will be!" I was determined to set a good example even if I had to do it on my own! I wanted to live in a way that would not disappoint others who might one day look up to me. If people were going to look at me, I wanted them to say without any hesitation, "That right there. That is how God intended us to live!" I firmly resolved to fight the good fight.

Even though I was lonely with no friends, I still had God with me. I would recite my little prayer in my most difficult and painful moments, "The Lord is my shepherd, there is *nothing* I shall want! The Lord is the center of my life." This would give me the strength to keep going. We would fight together!

BACKSLIDING

The school year ended, and I was on a spiritual high! My life seemed better than ever. I knew it was because I was living for God. I was removing from my life everything that made me displeasing to Him. My drinking and partying became extremely rare. If I did go out, I kept the drinking to a minimum, which made me very proud of myself.

In spite of my successes, I knew my summer was going to be challenging. I was very worried about what I would do around my older brother. For the first time in about seven years, he and I would have the opportunity to spend a lot of time together.

I called him when I got home for the summer to see what he was doing over the weekend. He invited me to the bars with him and his friends. I thought I could go hang out with them and limit myself to one or two drinks. Can you guess what happened? Uhhhh! The first outing was a complete disaster! When we got to the bar, my brother bought me a drink. I thought, "Okay, this is fine, but then that is it! No more after this one." Within five minutes my brother's friends started yelling, "Hey everybody! It is little Seany's twenty-first birthday! Yeahhhhhh!" Everyone around us started buying me drinks and wishing me a happy birthday. It wasn't actually my birthday, but my brother and his friends thought it would be funny if they told everyone it was. I didn't have the courage to say no to them buying me drinks.

In spite of this disaster, I still thought I could keep to my original plan. I figured they got that out of their system, and it wouldn't happen again. We all went out again the following weekend. Much to my surprise the same thing happened. In fact, it kept happening. It wasn't always my "birthday," but they continued to buy me drink after drink and hand them to me.

Now that I am older I can look back, analyze what happened, and see the hidden motivations that compelled me to keep taking their drinks. This may sound strange to you, but there is a part of me that has a hard time wasting things. If I thought I was going to waste some kind of food or drink, I would often consume it instead of throw it away. When someone bought me a drink and put it in my hand, I actually felt obligated to finish it. I felt I would be wasting their money if I didn't drink it. Wasting money bothered me because we never had much of it while I was growing up. Lastly, I let my pride motivate me to prove that I could drink as much as, or more than, they could. After a few weekends of absolute failure, I stopped going out with them. Even though I really wanted to be with my brother, I had to accept the fact that I could not go to the bars with them. I had to find some other way for us to spend time together.

Although I had difficulty standing up to my brother and his friends, I had no problem telling my old high school classmates that I would not drink. As a result, I lost every friend I ever had in my hometown. My new way of life conflicted with theirs, and they didn't want me around. I guess it bothered their consciences. I think I became a constant reminder of how we should be living. Rather than change their behavior they removed me from their lives just as they had snuffed out the voices of their own consciences. I didn't let it bother me because I wanted to do what was right in God's eyes. My summer concluded with several weeks of solid sobriety.

When my senior year of college started, my backsliding resumed. My biggest problem was the negative influence of one of my new roommates. He was very big into getting drunk and partying. He constantly talked about all the parties we were going to have. He even brought an extra refrigerator to our apartment that held a keg in it and had a beer tap on the front. I didn't want to get involved with the parties, but I also didn't want to feel left out. As a result, I joined in on the drinking throughout the first two months of school. I went to parties with my roommates, but the parties always left me feeling very unsatisfied and unfulfilled.

Around this time, something happened that has been vividly burned into my memory. It was the first time that I simply left a party and went home alone. I left because of Jesus. He was all I could think about the whole time I was there. As I looked around at my surroundings, I realized that it was not a place that Jesus would like me to be. Even after I reached my apartment, I was still talking to God and thinking about how He expected me to live. This was the first time I had ever thought about God or prayed to Him after having a few drinks. I knew that this meant my life was changing, and that my drinking days were coming to a close. I knew that God had become so much a part of my life that these empty activities would never satisfy me. They would only leave me sad and empty.

I want to interject something here as a side note. About five years after I left college, I thought about the morality of drinking alcohol. For many years after college, I had thought alcohol was purely evil, and that we should not touch it at all. Studying Jesus changed my opinion. He turned jugs of water into wine for a wedding feast so that people could drink it and celebrate. He also drank wine with His Apostles at the Last Supper before turning it into His own blood. These details made me realize that drinking alcohol was not a sin. This caused me to question why the government made a law that prohibits everyone under the age of twenty-one from drinking alcohol. I came to realize that the government is saying, "The use of this substance requires maturity and responsibility. It is a mind-altering substance, which requires good judgment. We think it takes someone at the maturity level of a twenty-one year old to handle it properly." The point is not to deprive younger people from having fun. The point is to give them a chance to grow up first. We all need a chance to mature so that we can make good decisions on how to properly use alcohol. Alcohol, in and of itself, is not sinful. It is how you use it that can become sinful.

If you look at my life and the lives of many other people, you can easily see that alcohol can be a doorway into a world of trouble. For this reason, you need to be extremely cautious of how you use it if you decide to try it when you are at the legal age.

The last point I'd like to make is that Jesus obeyed moral, civil laws as if God the Father imposed them. Jesus said that Pontius Pilate would have had no power over Him unless it had been given to him by His heavenly Father. In imitation of Jesus, we should obey civil laws, as long as they are morally correct. The bottom line is that we need to observe the legal drinking age. Even when it becomes legal for us, we should be moderate if we decide to drink alcohol. We should be very careful to *not* abuse our bodies with it.

IS IT ALL WORTH IT?

This next event happened during the winter, but I can't remember which month. To help you understand how out of the ordinary this event was, I'll tell you a few things about how I grew up. When my parents or teachers told me to do something, I pretty much did it without questioning. I also woke up from sleep quickly and easily. My eyes opened before I even had a chance to formulate a thought. I usually didn't even need an alarm clock to wake me up.

On one particular afternoon, I laid down for a nap between classes and fell asleep. This part was perfectly normal for me. It was how I woke up that was out of character. When I woke up, I became completely aware of everything around me, but for some reason I never opened my eyes. Questions started to run through my mind like, "What if there is no difference between heaven and hell? What if they don't even exist? What if it doesn't matter how I live now? What if I am wasting my time with all of this effort? What if I am doing all of this for no reason?" These thoughts surprised me. I had always just accepted the fact that there is a heaven and a hell, and that it matters how we live our lives here on earth. This is what I was taught, and I never questioned it.

The unpredictability of the situation continued. In the blink of an eye, I found myself standing on the top of a mountain. There was a large tree to my right. Its branches extended out over the hillside in front of me. I could only see about twenty feet down the mountainside in front of me before it sloped off so steeply that I couldn't see the rest of the mountainside or the valley below. A red ball flew up from the valley as if it had been launched from a catapult. It landed about fifteen feet in front of me and began to emit red smoke. The more the smoke came out, the darker it became. An overwhelming spooky feeling accompanied the smoke. I knew it represented the presence of evil. The more smoke there was, the more evil I felt.

With each passing moment, I became more and more afraid. I began to desperately search for help with my eyes. I gazed up and saw a brilliant, light-blue sky with hundreds of stars symmetrically placed three dimensionally across the horizon. The stars were sparkling white lights much like candle flames. There were soft white clouds floating in the background around the top of a beautiful snowcapped mountain. The scene was obviously from God. It represented heaven. I began to smile and said, "Please come Lord!" At that moment, I felt peaceful and happy. I felt like I could just float away and be at rest.

As I gazed in awe at this scenic vision, the sound of a violent destructive wind began to develop. It seemed like the noise was coming from behind the scene in front of me. Then a hole bore through the center of the sky, much like a drill bit boring through the bottom of a wooden board. The hole increased in size as evil issued forth in streaks of gray, black, and red. Among the streaks of color were varying sizes of solid black and gray debris. The stream of darkness grew in strength as it engulfed the sky.

This storm of darkness was headed straight for me. The closer it came, the louder and more powerful the violent winds became. I began to feel my clothes being pressed up against my body. My hair and the sleeves of my T-shirt also began to flap vigorously from the violent wind. My eardrums were pounded by the noise. I felt like I was standing in a vicious hurricane. Chunks of debris began to hit me in the face and body, which caused me to flinch. There was nowhere to run and nothing I could do to protect myself. The darkness was going to completely overtake me. I was terrified!

Just when I thought I was going to be destroyed, a gentle breeze began to blow from behind me. It completely overpowered the loud, vicious, evil storm and drove it back. The storm decreased in size and strength as it went. It looked like the same scene was being played in reverse. The hole that the evil had come out of decreased in size as it was pushed back through. In a matter of seconds, the picture of peace and tranquility was completely restored, and I felt calm again. I was left standing on the mountaintop with a gentle breeze blowing at my back and a beautiful picture in front of me. I knew that the breeze coming from behind me meant that God would always "have my back" to protect me. I also knew without any doubt that there *is* a heaven; there is a hell, and it does matter how I live my life here on earth. I knew that heaven is a beautiful, peaceful place filled with tranquility. Hell is a frightening place filled with fear, terror, pain, darkness, and destructive evil. I knew that my efforts to change were well worth it. Just as the smoke from the red ball grew darker as it came out, I understood that the longer I let evil be around me, the stronger its presence would be in my life. This meant I needed to keep away from evil influences as much as possible.

BE A SAINT

As the spring semester of my senior year began, I became aware of something that was happening inside of me. No words were involved. No one said anything, but somehow I just knew that God was asking me to become a Saint. He was referring to the kind of Saint that I had learned about in Catholic school growing up. The thought of becoming a Saint of that caliber petrified me because they all *suffered a lot*! I thought I would have to suffer greatly for the rest of my earthly life if I were to accept this challenge.

My image of Sainthood did not fit into the plans I had for my life. I just wanted to have a simple, quiet, happy, married life with no major problems, challenges, or sufferings. I wanted to be an all around average guy with no frills. I wanted to slip through life unnoticed. The way I saw it, Saints had to do big, important things. They stood out as examples for everyone else to follow. They were called to be heroic role models.

Since the concept of Sainthood did not fit into the plans I had for my life, I chose to ignore it. This didn't work because the idea would *not* go away. This calling nagged at my insides for days until I finally addressed it.

I considered my life on earth and my life throughout all eternity. Life on earth seemed so short compared to never-ending eternity. I thought, "How will I prepare for eternity? What I do now will determine where I will be after I die." I realized that I would only get one chance at life on earth. Jesus said that our choices and actions can have merit. He encouraged us to live a life which earned merit. By doing so, we would store up our treasures in heaven. It seemed obvious to me that the best choice was to store up treasures in heaven that will last forever. With much fear and trembling at what might be in store for me, I said, "Yes Lord, I will do it. I will be a Saint."

A YEAR GONE BY

A year had passed since the death of my cousin and the breakup with my fiancé. I had changed so much over that year. I had found true happiness by getting involved with my Church and living my life for God. God had also revealed to me that I was in the right Church by proving to me that Jesus is truly present in the Eucharist.

As the year progressed, the Eucharist had become the absolute center of my faith and relationship with Jesus. I had made it my priority to go to daily Mass so that I could physically receive Jesus every single day. By doing this, I continuously invited Him into my life to be my personal Lord and Savior. I couldn't understand how anyone who believed that Jesus is truly present in the Eucharist would not make it a priority to be at Church every single day to receive Him if they could. At the same time, I had become very bothered by people at Sunday Mass who were careless and irreverent toward Jesus in the Eucharist. I wanted to stand up and yell, "Don't you people realize what is going on here? Don't you realize you are standing in the presence of Almighty God? Can't you be a little more attentive and respectful?"

It wasn't until many years later that I realized I used to act just like the people I was judging. It wasn't until God changed my life that I started to be more attentive and respectful at Mass. If it were not for God's intervention, I probably never would have changed. This helped me realize that I needed to stop judging others. I had to realize that maybe God just hadn't touched their lives yet, and it is not totally their fault that they don't realize what is going on. Only God knows why people act the way they do. Since I don't know what someone's life has been like, I should not judge them. I was beginning to understand why Jesus said, "Judge not and you will not be judged." (Luke 6:37)

This picture was taken of me at a wedding during this time period. You can tell I had changed just by looking into my eyes.

THE ATTACK

As I increased my efforts to be good, I started to realize that I was frequently being attacked by the devil. Up until this point in my life I didn't think the devil even knew who I was. I thought that if I just lived a quiet life and didn't do anything noticeable, he wouldn't bother me. The *fact* is that he has known me and taunted me throughout my life. I just never realized the devil was attacking me because he attacks in ways I never expected him to. No one ever told me he could plant thoughts in my head. I came to learn about it on my own through the difficult experiences I am about to explain.

It started happening one day as I was walking to class. Loud, vicious, judgmental thoughts started *pounding* me in the head every time I looked at someone. They were much stronger and more violent than a normal thought. There was a lot of anger and hatred behind them. They were things like, "YOU'RE FAT! YOU'RE UGLY! NO ONE IS EVER GOING TO LOVE YOU! NO ONE IS EVER GOING TO WANT YOU! THAT IS THE STUPIDEST HAIRCUT I HAVE EVER SEEN!" These thoughts didn't just pass through my mind. They literally *pounded* into my head with a strong force.

Every time my eyes focused on someone I received another one of these pounding, negative thoughts. I started closing my eyes or looking down at the ground in order to avoid making eye contact with people. I cried out to God for help! I prayed fervently asking God to take these thoughts away from me. I wrestled with them every day as I walked to and from class. This arduous conflict lasted for two weeks before God finally granted me a tremendous gift to overcome them.

I was walking up the hill for daily Mass when it happened. A judgmental thought came flying at my head like a hammer. I could actually feel it coming and braced myself to withstand the moment of impact. Without even thinking, I uttered out loud in a soft, soothing, long, and drawn-out way, "Shhhhh." With that, a deep peace came over my whole being, and the thought completely dissolved into nothing. This surprised me and made me smile. The sound was so soft yet so powerful. From that moment on, whenever a judgmental thought came at me, I would gently say, "Shhhhh." Every time I said it, a sense of peace would come over me, and the evil thought would be completely crushed. Before long, the judgmental thoughts tapered off and stopped bothering me completely.

Years later I reflected back on this experience as well as my experience of coming to believe that Jesus is truly present in the Eucharist. I could clearly see how the devil had pounded thoughts into my head in both situations. He caused me to feel tremendous strain, guilt, doubt, and a lack of peace through using these thoughts against me.

My message to you is this; *be aware of your thoughts! They don't all come from you.* Learn which ones are actually yours and which ones are not. Act on the good ones and reject the bad ones.

TESTIMONY

There was a prayer group meeting the following Saturday night, which I attended. I had successfully made it to every meeting that year. When it came time for the "faith sharing" segment of the meeting, my heart started pounding profusely. It felt like it was going to jump right out of my chest. A strange tingly feeling came over me, and it wouldn't go away. The thought came to me that I should get up and tell everyone what happened with the judgmental thoughts. It was an awkward yet powerful moment.

While my soul was going through a new and intense experience, I was fearfully thinking, "NO! DON'T GET UP IN FRONT OF EVERYONE!" It seemed like the only way I would be able to calm the intense, heart-pounding feeling would be to get up and speak. An uncomfortable stillness filled the room. No one was getting up to share their testimony. It almost seemed as if the Holy Spirit was holding the floor open for me.

With great hesitation I began to stand. I looked up to the front of the Chapel and began walking. When I reached the front of the Chapel, I turned around to see that everyone was intently staring at me. In the utter silence of the room, I frantically questioned myself, "What am I going to say?" As I stood there motionless and speechless, someone yelled out, "Tell us your name!" With a slight stutter, I said, "Mmm, my name is Sean McVeigh." After a brief pause, I said, "I never did this before." Before I could say another word, everyone started clapping in support of me. When they had finished, I slowly opened my mouth to speak. "I am not sure how to explain this, but I just had an interesting experience these past few weeks." I proceeded to explain the whole battle I had with the evil, judgmental thoughts and how I had received a gift from the Holy Spirit using the sound of "Shhhh" to defeat them. Everyone clapped for me when I finished, and I walked back to my seat. I was really embarrassed and felt like a complete idiot after telling people what I had gone through. I was afraid they were all going to think I was crazy.

Several of the people who were at the prayer meeting approached me a few days later at Mass. They told me they were able to use my gift of "Shhhh" with great success against nasty thoughts they were having. It made me happy to think that God actually used my testimony to help them. It also gave me a sense of relief to know that they didn't think I was crazy. Instead, they actually admired me, which was nice.

After I spoke with those students, I talked to the group's advisor about the strange intense feeling I had before getting up to give my testimony. She explained that it was the Holy Spirit revealing to me that I was the one being called to give a testimony. I thought the whole experience was really neat. I liked being chosen by the Holy Spirit to get up in front of everyone to give a message that would help them.

RETREAT

One thing that I really wanted to do during my last year at Penn State was go on a spiritual retreat. With four months left in the school year, I signed up for the next retreat that was offered by the Penn State Catholic Community. It was called a "Revival Retreat." I was so determined to go that nothing could stop me, not even the eight inches of snow that fell the day the retreat was scheduled to start. Forty students had signed up for the retreat, but only fifteen ended up going because of the storm.

Not much happened at first because the priest was a few hours late in getting there. He had to drive all the way from New Jersey, which would have taken about four hours on a good day. Since it was snowing like crazy, and he wasn't sure where he was going, it ended up taking him eight hours to get there. Things quickly changed after he arrived. We praised and worshiped God together. Many of the students were using the Charismatic Gifts of the Holy Spirit.

In between praise and worship sessions, the priest gave us inspirational talks about the gifts and workings of the Holy Spirit. I was filled with a million questions, and I was burning for a chance to ask him some of them. I sat directly across from him during dinner the next day, hoping I would have an opportunity to ask him some of my questions. I didn't want to interrupt him during the meal, so I waited until he finished eating. Before I had a chance to talk to him, he stood up to leave the table. I didn't do it out loud, but in my mind I screamed, "NO! DON'T GO! I NEED TO TALK TO YOU!" As those thoughts fired through my mind, he turned and looked straight at me. Without taking his eyes off of me, he slowly and smoothly handed his plate off to someone, and then slowly sat back down. It seemed as if he somehow heard my thoughts and responded to them. I immediately said, "Father, I need to ask you some questions."

I proceeded to ask him question after question about God and the workings of the Holy Spirit. With each answer he gave, I felt more and more alive and fulfilled. I felt like I was a cup, and the waters of the Holy Spirit were filling me up until I was overflowing with an amazing *joy*! My body was tingly and utterly filled with so much life, love, and peace. After our conversation ended, I ran around the entire retreat house with intense excitement giving everyone a big hug. I wanted them all to feel as great as I felt.

The retreat was very special. I had been waiting for more than a year, and God finally answered my prayer for some religious friends. For the first time in my life, I felt deeply loved by people. I felt like I suddenly had a loving family filled with amazing brothers and sisters! After that retreat, I felt so fulfilled and content in life! This was a feeling that I never had before, and it was the best feeling I could have imagined. It enabled me to realize that there is a difference between just hearing someone say the words "I love you," and actually feeling loved by them. That was the biggest unspoken lesson I learned from the retreat. I was happy living my life for God throughout the past year, but I experienced an even greater happiness and fulfillment when I felt loved by other people as well.

WEEKLY PRAYER GROUP MEETINGS

Many of the people on the retreat were members of a Charismatic prayer group that met every Tuesday night in the Catholic Chapel on campus. This was great news for me, and I started going every week. Before long, we decided to start a second prayer group that would meet on Wednesday nights. The advisor of the Tuesday night prayer group asked me to be the leader of the new Wednesday night group. I didn't feel ready or worthy to lead the meetings because I was so new to the whole prayer group scene. No one else was willing to do it though, so I ended up accepting the responsibility despite my inner hesitation.

I began to feel inspired to look for other areas of my life that I had not given to God. There was one TV show in particular that I really liked, but it had many negative and ungodly messages regarding sex. They portrayed sex outside of marriage as acceptable and more like a sport than something sacred. Although it was difficult, I forced myself to stop watching it.

I also looked at my music collection. Many of the songs I liked carried bad messages and used foul language. I chose to get rid of all my old music and forced myself to listen to only Christian worship music. This was hard for me to do at first because a lot of the Christian music wasn't exactly my style. Over time it began to grow on me, and I learned to like it. I chose to make this decision because I *wanted* to be totally devoted to God.

Going to Mass, listening to worship music, and praising God had become such a joy in my life that I even began waking up in the middle of the night from singing worship songs in my sleep. There was always a huge smile on my face when this happened, and it made me feel happy to be living for God. I began to realize that the music I used to listen to, and the TV shows I used to watch, never made me this happy. They only temporarily entertained me. I realized that those forms of entertainment had distracted me from finding true happiness. My new way of life made me feel amazingly fulfilled. At times, I would feel so much love inside of me that I thought my heart might actually explode. Sometimes this powerful feeling of love would carry on night and day for several weeks without stopping. It was so intense that I sometimes wondered if I was having some form of prolonged heart attack.

I can say without any doubt that this was the best time of my life! It felt like I was living heaven on earth! I found everything I ever wanted in God, daily Mass, and the prayer groups I attended. Most of the prayer group members were the same Catholics who went to daily Mass, but some were from other religious denominations. I loved the fact that we were united in our common love for Jesus Christ and our desire to live the Gospel. We didn't let differences in theology come between us. We simply focused on loving one another as brothers and sisters in Christ.

My new friends and I didn't stop at just meeting on Tuesday and Wednesday nights for prayer. We also started gathering every Friday and Saturday night for unofficial prayer group meetings. Two of the members were husband and wife, both of whom were in graduate school. They lived in a little cottage along a stream about ten minutes away from campus. We met there for our weekend worship sessions.

WHICH PATH WILL YOU FOLLOW?

When I left town on the weekend nights to go to these meetings, I saw thousands of students already drunk or getting drunk. The back alleys in town were filled with unsettling yelling and screaming. The students were all searching for the same thing I had been searching for when I was in their position. They wanted to be truly happy and accepted by others. They wanted to have fun and feel good.

They were making the same mistake I had made before God stepped in and helped me change my life. They were trying to find happiness, fun, acceptance, and good feelings by doing things that often lead to sin. This was especially true when drinking alcohol was involved. Drinking alcohol can make you feel tingly, but it is not the kind of feeling that fulfills you or makes you truly happy.

A lot of people drink because they are insecure and are trying to fit in with others. Some do it to lower their inhibitions and overcome the inner fears they subconsciously feel around people. Some do it because they think it makes them funny. Alcohol becomes their crutch and an excuse for their actions. One of the problems with this is that, although their senses and ability to think clearly are taken away by drinking, the consequences of their actions are not taken away. For example, the more people drink and lose their senses, the more they think they can drink. This is how many people end up drinking until they become violently ill.

Feeling sick and hung over is the consequence of their bad choices. Some people even end up pregnant or with a disease from getting drunk and sleeping with someone. Some people don't mature emotionally because they rely on substances like alcohol rather than authentic inner courage to overcome their personal fears. Some people end up killed or critically injured in traumatic accidents just like I was when I was seventeen! Please don't be foolish and think that bad things could never happen to you if you drink. I never thought about the consequences of being around alcohol. Yet, look at all the pain it caused me! Is that what you want?

I never found *true* happiness or acceptance from others when I went out drinking and partying. At times I may have told myself I was having fun, but that wasn't the truth deep down in my heart. Parties left me feeling empty and alone inside. Much to my surprise, I found true happiness through giving my best effort at Church, praising God, and hanging out with other people who wanted to love and serve God. My religious friends made me feel truly accepted for who I was as a person regardless of what I said or did. They made me feel like I was part of a big family.

You need to realize that you have a choice to make in your search for true happiness. Which path will you follow? The one that leads to God and inner fulfillment, or the one that leads to self-destruction? Please don't read any further until you spend some time thinking about the choices you will make in your search for true happiness.

BLAST FROM THE PAST

One Friday evening in the spring I headed over to the couple's cottage for our weekend praise, worship, and fellowship session. As usual, I was feeling high on life! They were watching the movie "Jesus of Nazareth" when I arrived. The scene where Jesus is scourged at the pillar was on as I walked in the door.

The moment I saw the Roman soldiers slashing Jesus with their whips, I became clearly aware of two very serious areas of sin from my past that I had never confessed. One of them in particular deeply bothered me. When I was a young boy, I had stolen a bunch of candy from a concession stand across the street from our house. I felt so bad and guilty that I hid the sin in the back of my mind and never told anyone about it. The other area of sin that came to my mind was sexual sins I had committed in the past but had not repented for. Up until that moment I had only come to terms with having sex with the girls I mentioned earlier in this book, but there were other sexual sins I was guilty of. I had forced myself to completely forget about them. I must have thought that forgetting about them would erase them from my life, and I would never have to face them again. When I saw Jesus getting whipped, I became painfully aware that it was through those sins that I had scourged Him too. He took my sins onto Himself in order to save me from hell. I didn't like the thought of hurting Him. I felt so bad for committing those sins. I wanted to run out the door and immediately go to Confession, but I had to wait until four o'clock the next day when the local Church was having Confessions.

The following day I avoided everyone and walked to the Church where Confessions were being held. It took me about forty-five minutes to get there. I remember the exact clothes I was wearing and everything. They were a pair of black jeans and a thick, soft, white sweatshirt with black and red lettering on the front. It was sunny but cool outside, which made it great weather for walking.

Three priests were hearing Confessions when I arrived at the Church. I picked the shortest line and got into it. My hands were slightly shaking from nervousness as I prepared myself to say out loud the things that I never ever, ever, ever wanted to tell anyone else in the whole wide world with the exception of my wife. I wanted to share everything about myself with her.

The next thing I knew the person in front of me came out of the confessional. It was my turn. I went in and looked around as I pulled the door closed behind me. The walls were covered with thick white carpeting to dampen the sound, so that no one in the Church could hear what was being said in the confessional. There was a kneeler on the floor to my right. I had to turn my body ninety degrees in order to use it. Directly in front of the kneeler was a wall with a white screen in the middle of it. When I reached the kneeling position, I looked up to see that the white screen was directly in front of my face. A priest was sitting on the other side of it. The *major problem* was that I could see right through the screen, and the priest could see me. "Oh no! He sees me!" I screamed in my mind. Beads of sweat covered the backs of my legs and poured down my chest and back. All of this happened in a matter of seconds. With intense anxiety I pushed myself through the standard opening of the Sacrament of Penance. Then, with a gut-wrenching strain, I quickly told him my horrible sins. I braced myself for the severe penance the priest was going to give me. This was the part I was most afraid of. As I winced and prepared myself for his reaction, he calmly said, "You have made a good Confession today. For your penance say one Our Father. Now make an Act of Contrition." I was shocked and thought to myself, "That's it? That is all I have to do, one Our Father?" In an instant, I felt completely set free by God. These sins that I had carried and kept hidden from my own mind and from everyone else were now lifted. I had faced them, and God forgave me.

After saying my Act of Contrition, I went out into the Church to do my easy penance. As I knelt down, I noticed the feeling of cool air against the sweat that completely covered my body. My face was plastered with a massive smile, and I was filled with *joy* from going to the Sacrament of Penance and being forgiven. Having to pray only *one* Our Father as a penance made me feel like God was saying to me, "What seemed like the end of the world to you is no big deal to Me. I just wanted you to come and be set free. I wanted to take your sins away from you so that you wouldn't have to carry them anymore." I finished my prayer and floated home filled with peace. I wished I could capture that amazing feeling and keep it with me all day long every day!

The devil plays on the feelings we get from committing a sin and tries to convince us to keep the sin hidden. When we keep a sin hidden, we stay in his bondage. It is easier for him to manipulate us and our thoughts when we live in the bondage of sin. Jesus understood our human condition and our need to confess our sins. This is why He established the Sacrament of Penance in the Gospel of John 20:22-23. He did this by enabling the Apostles, through the power of the Holy Spirit, to forgive a sin after they heard a person's confession. In the fifth chapter of the book of James, we are told to confess our sins to one another and pray for one another that we may receive healing. The key point is to confess your sins rather than keep them hidden.

It is possible for us to stuff our past sins so far down into our souls that we totally forget about them. But that doesn't take them away or make us feel any better. *It is simply **not** the right way to deal with sins.* In fact, those sins will periodically come up in your life until you deal with them properly. I hope that every reader who has a sin they have not yet repented for will confess it, so that they can be properly reconciled with God and feel set free!

I also hope you realize from my example that God is patient with us. He dealt with me in stages. When I first went back to the Sacrament of Penance, it seemed like the only big sin I needed to confess was sex with Kim. God waited until I was more emotionally and spiritually ready to handle the rest of the bad sins I had suppressed before He brought them to the front of my mind, so that I could deal with them properly. I make this point because I want you to see clearly that even someone who feels God's presence in their life, and is trying very hard to follow Him, may still have sins they need to address, confess, and repent for. What are the sins in your life that you still need to deal with?

THE WAY TO ME

Near the end of the school year, I was kneeling on the Chapel floor praying. It was early in the morning. All the lights were off. The sun was just starting to rise, dimly lighting the Chapel through the stained glass window. This created a mystical feeling. As I silently knelt there with my eyes closed, I suddenly had an inner vision. The interesting thing about this vision was that I was physically in it and could sense what was going on around me in the vision. I found myself kneeling at the feet of Jesus. I excitedly thought, "Wow, I made it! I finally made it to Jesus!" I became curious. I wanted to know what His face looked like. I began to raise my head *very slowly*. My eyes moved upward over His white robe. Anticipation began to build as my line of sight approached His shoulders. Before my eyes reached His face, I noticed that His right arm was extended. Without even thinking about it, my head turned and followed down His arm. When I reached His hand I could see that His finger was pointing at something. I automatically turned my head in the direction He was pointing, and my eyes came to rest on the Blessed Virgin Mary. The moment I laid eyes on her, Jesus spoke to me saying, "If you want to get close to Me, you must come through her." I snapped out of the vision as I yelled, "No!"

Clearly, I did not like Jesus' statement. I just wanted to go straight to Jesus Himself. I didn't want to have to go through anyone else to get to Him. At first I refused to go through Mary. I thought that she would come between Jesus and me. I thought that praying the rosary would take my focus off Jesus. I was afraid I would then slip back into my former lifestyle and fall away from God completely. I was petrified of losing my newfound relationship with Jesus. My ultimate fear was that I would end up in hell if I took my attention off Jesus for even a second.

Over time I began to realize that I was not getting any closer to Jesus. The thought of approaching Him through Mary continued to gnaw at my mind. The concept kept presenting itself to me. Most of the very famous Saints I had been reading about at that time, such as St. Louis De Montfort, approached Jesus through Mary.

One of the things I remember hearing at that time was, "No one knows a son better than the mother who raised him." After seriously pondering this concept, I began to realize that Mary probably knew Jesus better than any other human. After all, she lived with Jesus Christ Himself for about thirty years. THIRTY YEARS! No other human being can make that claim. She nursed Him as an infant and watched Him play as a child. She watched Him eat, sleep, talk, cry, breathe, and interact with their neighbors. She saw the way He acted in every situation. She observed His entire development as a person. I compared her thirty years with Jesus to the three years that the Apostles had spent with Him.

Thirty years is a long time! Once I came to terms with the idea that Mary must have known Jesus better than anyone else, I reluctantly started talking to her and praying the rosary. By giving her a chance, I learned that my preconceived notions about her and the rosary were wrong.

I had always thought that the rosary was about Mary. What I quickly learned was that the rosary is primarily a meditation on the life, death, and resurrection of Jesus Christ. I found that it gave me spiritual insight into Jesus' life that I never would have seen if I had not prayed the rosary and asked Mary to open my eyes.

Here is an example of one of the many things I learned about Jesus. The book of Hebrews states that, even though Jesus was God, He *learned obedience* through what He suffered. Jesus actually had to learn how to be obedient. I came to understand what this passage meant as I pondered the Fifth Joyful Mystery of the rosary. In this mystery, Joseph and Mary find Jesus in the temple after He had been missing for three days. When Jesus saw how His actions upset Joseph and Mary, He in turn felt hurt. It was this pain, this emotional suffering, that taught Him how to be humanly obedient to His parents. After He allowed His emotions to teach Him in this situation, the Scripture says that He went with Joseph and Mary and was *obedient* to them (Luke 2:51). In this situation, He learned obedience through what He emotionally suffered.

Picking up on aspects of Jesus' life from praying the rosary helped me see new ways that I needed to change. I just wish I had understood how to let my emotions teach me while I was growing up in the same way Jesus did. I would have avoided a lot of unnecessary pain in life if I had only been more obedient to my parents and my Church's teachings.

As you can probably see through this one example, praying the rosary and talking with Mary turned out quite the opposite of what I expected. I began to know Jesus much more intimately. I grew to have a deeper insight into the spiritual life. This helped me imitate aspects of Jesus' life that I never would have noticed had I not prayed the rosary.

I also started to see that Jesus wanted me to respect His mother just as He had done while He was on earth and still does in heaven. Getting to know Mary also helped my concept of God and His family become much *more realistic* and *less militant*. This is probably one of the main reasons why Jesus made me approach Him through Mary. Before getting to know Mary, I was so focused on Jesus that I didn't view Mary, the Saints, and many of the people on earth as my true family. Speaking to Mary helped me realize that we are all in this together, which broadened my view of reality. We truly are one big family. We need to support and encourage one another and help each other grow.

I encourage you, the reader, to grow in your prayer life and develop your understanding of what it means to be a member of God's family. Having a strong prayer life becomes particularly important when you are facing hard times or temptations. Praying through those situations by calling on God and your spiritual family will help you embrace God's grace and make better decisions. Praying will also help you realize what situations you should avoid. Avoiding a bad situation is far easier than trying to make the right decision after you are already under pressure.

CONCLUSION

Before I conclude this book, I want to thank you for taking the time to read it. If you are one of those people who jump ahead to the conclusion before reading the content of a book, I ask you to please be disciplined and save the conclusion until *after* you have read through the entire story.

I hope that you have learned many valuable life lessons by observing my successes and failures and how God interacted with me through them. Keep in mind that the key theme of this book is: "I've got to change!" I've got to *choose* to turn away from my sinful ways and become a better person in God's eyes.

The whole reason why I've gone through the trouble to tell you about all the ways that I've got to change is so that you will think about all the ways that you've got to change. In order to help you with this task, I have filled this conclusion with a tremendous amount of information and insight. To maximize the effectiveness of this section, I encourage you to take your time and give a lot of attention to each paragraph. You may even find it helpful to read certain sections several times.

To start off, if there is anything in particular that God wants you to work on changing right now in your life it will probably come to your mind after sincerely asking yourself, "If I would have died today, would I have gone to heaven?" It is up to you to change that aspect of your life. If nothing comes to mind, then take a good look at your life and pick out the things you'd most like to improve. Formulate a game plan, and then get to work on them.

The things that I had to work on the most while I was in high school and college were: cheating on tests, missing Church on Sunday, sexual sins, alcohol, negative use of foul language, and giving in to negative peer pressures. What are the most challenging areas in your life right now?

It often takes a tremendous amount of effort to overcome your inner emotions and peer pressure in order to do the right thing.

Take note how hard it was for me to overcome my weaknesses and sinfulness even though I was putting forth a strong effort. Imagine how much more destructive those things can be in your life if you are not trying to *change.*

If you make a mistake, it is really important to deal with it the right way. Be watchful of your human tendency to lie to yourself and everyone else around you. We tend to want to hide our sins and rationalize them. That only gives the devil a chance to influence our thoughts. Once he gets a foothold in our minds, he will try to pull us further down the wrong path.

The devil also tries to convince us that going to Confession isn't talked about in the Bible, but it is. Don't listen to the devil, and please don't make the same mistake I did and think that telling God your sins in private is enough. It wasn't until I started going to Confession *with a sincere heart* that I experienced deep forgiveness from God and joy from the Holy Spirit. My experiences have taught me that *going to Confession truly **is** the best way to deal with sin.* I encourage you to make it your discipline to confess your sins with deep sincerity as soon as possible. Be authentic and honest! Don't try to make it sound good. Just tell a priest your sins and get the job done!

Even though I sometimes feel afraid of what the priest will think of me, I *push* myself to say my sins out loud anyway. It is when I do this that I feel truly set free and forgiven by God. I also like to go face to face with a priest because it really helps me avoid committing that sin again. The next time I'm tempted with that sin I simply think of how embarrassing it will feel to look the priest in the face and tell him that I just committed the same sin again. That thought alone has helped me say *no way* to various temptations I've faced in life! Talking about your sins also gives you a chance to figure out *why* you did it in the first place. You can then develop a plan to deal with it, avoid it in the future, and grow as a person.

I think sometimes God allows us to feel the pain our sins cause in order to help us avoid making that same mistake again. The next time we are tempted with that sin we can think back to the pain it caused us and say *no thanks*! I'm not doing that again! This way of thinking will be especially important after you have had a long time of success in living the right way. As I look back at my own life, I realize that I would correct my ways in dealing with sexual sins for about six months. After that amount of time, my hurt feelings would fade into the background. Then I would meet a girl that I really wanted to hold on to. My desires and insecurities would take over, and I would fall into sin trying to hold on to a girl who really wasn't meant to be mine in the first place. I never even realized that I was letting my emotions and insecurities run my life. I strongly encourage you to learn to recognize your inner fears and insecurities. Learn how to overcome them in order to make the right decisions. Sometimes just reminding yourself of all the pain and long-term negative consequences that sin can cause is enough to motivate you to do the right thing.

It is obvious that sex outside of marriage is wrong, but it is important to acknowledge that there are other sexual sins that we must avoid such as "fooling around" and masturbation. By "fooling around" I mean touching and fondling someone else's private areas. Sex is supposed to be a time where you totally *give* yourself to the one you love. It is an act of *giving* not of *taking*. "Fooling around" is a form of taking; this is one of the main reasons why it is wrong. Masturbation is also an act of taking. In both of these situations, you are performing actions to take a good feeling for yourself, or to win someone over who is not meant to be yours in the first place.

You may be tempted to commit sexual sins based on your insecurity and desperation to hold on to someone. You may also be tempted to give in to someone else's pressure. You may be tempted with these sins because you want to fit in with everyone else who says they are doing them. You may be tempted out of curiosity. You may be tempted because you are looking for something that will make you feel good.

People who engage in *any* of these self-gratifying sinful activities usually don't realize that they are training themselves to be takers rather than people who give of themselves freely in love. The end result is that they never find deep love because they are so far removed from how to give of themselves correctly. That is one of the biggest hidden reasons why many marriages have failed. I hope you can see that it is not worth committing sexual sins because they only serve to *mess you up* in the bigger picture! I hope you will choose to have a more wholesome, giving, fulfilling, and loving life rather than one that is focused on taking brief moments of pleasure for yourself. Just remember that *the choice is yours to make*!

Dealing with sexual temptations may be one of the most difficult and painful choices you will have to continually make in your life. It is like Olympic athletes who give up eating dessert and junk food in order to train themselves to win a gold medal. If you are called to marriage, you can view your future marriage relationship as your gold medal. In order to win, you *must* deny yourself the immediate gratification that sexual sins offer just like athletes must deny themselves the immediate gratification of junk food. If you do not work hard and train yourself, you will *not* win the race. Instead, you will go home empty handed. Is that what you want?

If you have already been involved in these types of sins and are going through an emotionally painful breakup with someone, don't think that illegal drugs or alcohol are going to take away your pain. They only make matters worse! They don't actually remove the emotional pain. They leave you even more depressed than you were to begin with. You need to realize that the pain is going to stay there until you face it, deal with it properly, and patiently allow your heart to heal over time.

Emotional wounds need time to heal just like physical wounds do. For example, if you get a terrible, huge, abrasive cut on your arm, it isn't going to heal over night. You first need to clean it up. This is like going to Confession. Then the cut will form a scab. You have to be careful with the wound, tend to it, and change the bandages. When it comes to emotional wounds from sin, the ointments you need to use are prayer and talking about it with the right people. Over time the scab will shrink until finally the area is healed. There may be a scar which reminds you of the wound, but the healing process is complete. Emotional wounds will heal the same way if you don't pick at them and aggravate them with negative thoughts.

Overall, you need to be patient in dealing with emotional and spiritual wounds. Remember how my worst breakup turned into the best thing that ever happened to me. No matter how bad it hurts or how badly you wanted the relationship to work out, hold on to the belief that you will be better off in the long run just as I was.

While going through hard times, it may also help to think about Jesus hanging on the cross. His pain and suffering looked awful, and it appeared that nothing good could come out of it, but in the end He triumphantly rose to new life! You too will rise to new life! Whether it is through a deeper personal relationship with God, or through people He brings into your life, God will always provide, so don't think that this suffering is the end of the world.

At this point, I'd like to elaborate on the word, "CHOICE." You have the ability to make your own choices in life. Very often people make decisions based on emotion rather than on sound thinking. This leads to problems when your emotions are being influenced by impure thoughts or people who are *not* trying to lead you closer to God. The people *or* the thoughts trying to get you to do the wrong thing could sound something like, "Come on. Just do it. You only live once. No one will even know. It will just be this one time…"

Negative influences will play on your desires, emotions, and insecurities in a way that may make it difficult for you to think clearly and make the right choice. When this happens, you need to *focus hard* and think about the effects of your actions. Realize that there *are* consequences to the choices you make! In those moments, you *must push yourself* to do the right thing! If you find yourself thinking and praying a lot about a moral choice, then the answer is probably **No! Don't do it! Avoid the situation! Go home! Get out of there!**

An example of this is the girl who really wants to hold on to her boyfriend, but he is pressuring her to fool around or have sex. She spends many agonizing hours thinking about it. This is what I mean about spending a long time trying to figure out if you should do something or not. Rather than continuously agonize over it, she should stop and realize that the correct answer is simply **No! Don't do it!** She would be better off ending the relationship and waiting for someone who will authentically love and cherish her. To help her with this decision, she needs to accept that her current boyfriend does not authentically love her. If he did, he would want to sacrifice the immediate gratification of sex and fooling around. In fact, he would *not* even consider pressuring her with them if he truly loved her. If he is pressuring her, then he is attempting to *use* her to fulfill his own desires for immediate gratification; that's *not love*!

On the other hand, if you are the one who is trying to get someone to fool around with you or have sex with you, you need to realize that you are *not* listening to the voice of God! You need to change so that you don't end up in hell.

It is very important to learn how to pray during these types of situations and temptations. Ask God to help you choose wisely and overcome the people, thoughts, and feelings that are pushing you to make the wrong choice.

On the other end of the spectrum are the people and Church teachings that are encouraging you to do the right thing. At times they will tell you that you are not allowed to do something. It is unfortunate when "rules" are presented in ways that do not inspire you to follow them. The challenge for you will be to stay calm and not get upset by the way rules are presented. Instead, you should step back and realize that rules are there to help you make the right decision. Unfortunately, many young people make the *wrong* decision because they are thinking with their emotions, focusing on immediate gratification, and ignoring the long-term consequences. Some young people will even make a disobedient choice just to rebel against the people or person who gave them the rule. Very often the problem goes back to *how* the rule was presented and *not* the rule itself. To be most effective, a rule should be presented in a way that will help you understand *why* the forbidden action is wrong. It should also motivate you to be obedient.

Your job is to acknowledge when your emotions cause you to resist your parent's rules or the Church's teachings. For example, if your parent or guardian says to you, "You're not allowed to watch that movie," be careful to stay calm. Your immediate reaction may be to get upset and resent them because it feels like they are depriving you of something that other people are getting to do. This is also where the devil may throw thoughts into your head because he knows you are more susceptible to his influence at that moment. He'll play on your hurt feelings in an attempt to turn you against the person who upset you. The more he can turn you against them, the better his chances are at talking you into sinning.

Rather than keep all your thoughts bottled up in your head and risk letting the devil influence you, it is better to calmly and maturely talk with the person who gave you the rule. Tell them you understand that they gave you the rule because they care about you, but their way of presenting it has caused a conflict within your mind and emotions. Help them understand that their rule is difficult for you to deal with because many other people are getting to do it. It is possible that your parents or guardians need to work on how they present rules. Your talking to them may help them improve their technique.

Sometimes they just need to clearly explain *why* you are not supposed to do something. For example, I was always taught that sex outside of marriage is wrong, but no one ever took the time to clearly explain all the reasons *why* it is wrong. It wasn't until after I devastatingly hurt myself through having sex that God educated me as to *why* it is wrong. I strongly encourage you to go back and reread that section. Sometimes understanding *why* there is a rule can help you understand *why* it is in your best interest to obey it. The key is to listen to the voice of reason rather than peer pressure or the inner emotions that motivate you to make bad choices. I hope you can see from my example that it is much better to follow rules than it is to break them! Imitating Jesus by being obedient to your parents and to God the Father's plan can definitely help you avoid a lot of unnecessary suffering! Also, if there has ever been a time you were disobedient to your parents, I'd encourage you to apologize to them. It may even turn into a wholesome conversation which will help you to grow in a mutual respect for one another.

I hope you were able to clearly see from my story how the devil can plant thoughts in your mind. Among other things, these thoughts can leave you feeling strained, anxious, angry, lustful, or afraid. They are designed to ruin your inner peace or lead you into sin. Other people can also suggest sinful actions to you. I encourage you to go back and study the events that took place, and the thoughts I had, when I went out with my friend Brad during Lent on his 21st birthday. Study Brad's words and actions as well. He led me away from God, and so did my own thoughts. Learn to recognize when people are doing that to you. Also reread and study the thoughts I had when I was trying to be Catholic for one week and believe that Jesus is truly present in the Eucharist. Lastly, reread the time I was being attacked in my mind with judgmental thoughts of others, as I walked around my college campus.

Realize that there are basically two different *types* of thoughts you can have in your mind. There are those you have while *actively* thinking of something such as what you will eat for lunch. The other type of thought is the kind that just seems to *passively* pop into your mind. These two types of thoughts are clearly different, but few people have learned to distinguish between them. It is the type of thought that *passively* pops into your head that you need to analyze and determine where it came from. Did it come from your subconscious, God, the world (outside influences), or the devil? If you are not sure, it is best to avoid acting on the thought. Once you determine where it came from, you can choose to follow it or not. You may want to sit quietly and ponder this concept for a while before continuing on.

Next, I'd like you to think about TV shows, movies, internet, and music. All of these can have a positive *or* negative influence on your life. Even though you may like certain music and TV shows, you need to stop and think whether their messages are healthy or not. You need to realize that they *do* have an impact and influence on you. A perfect example of this is when I had just overcome my foul language problem and then watched an R rated movie at my parent's house. There was a tremendous amount of foul language in the movie. After it was over, I found myself saying bad words almost immediately. I also took on the same bad attitude portrayed by the character. I've even had nightmares after watching scary movies because they negatively influenced my subconscious. Has that ever happened to you? If so, I hope you are beginning to realize that these things *can* affect you.

My experiences have taught me that I need to make good choices in what I watch. For example, I recently watched a very funny TV show. I liked the personality of the characters and the close friendships they shared. Many of the aspects of the show appealed to my emotional side, which made me want to see it again. It was actually difficult to do, but I chose to not let myself watch that show again because all of the humor revolved around sexual sins. They made it sound like it is okay, normal, and even funny for people to have sex outside of marriage. Sex outside of marriage is *not* okay, and I need to protect myself from becoming desensitized to that message. We need to put our foot down and say No! Sex is simply wrong when it is done outside of marriage. It is wrong for two people to live together if they are not married. Sex outside of marriage plays with our emotions and messes us up! You can see this clearly after reading my story. Just because a TV show makes you laugh, or the beat in a song sounds good, it does not mean that the message is acceptable. You need to make choices for yourself about what you will allow into your life and what you will not.

Please *don't* be like the fools who think that TV, movies, internet, people, and music do not influence them. Foolish people never stop to ask themselves, is this good for me to watch? Is this good for me to listen to? Is this providing a healthy message? Is this video game something that Jesus would sit down and play with me, or is it too violent? Is this person helping me grow closer to God, or are they pulling me away from Him?

If you choose to be wise, instead of foolishly following the wrong emotions or bad influences, you will sometimes need to say to yourself: although I like this person, he or she is not good for me to be around, so I'm not going to hang out with them anymore. Although I may like the way this song sounds, I'm not going to listen to it anymore. There's too much foul language, and the lyrics give a bad message. I'm not going to visit that website because the pictures are inappropriate. I'm not going to watch this TV program because it is giving a bad message.

You can expect these decisions to be painful and difficult at times. There may be no immediate reward. It is only in the grand scheme of life and eternity that you will see the true benefits of making better choices for yourself and not letting the wrong people, negative outside influences, or improper inner emotions control your decisions.

Ultimately, only God can fill you with the happiness you desire. If you try to find fulfillment in games, entertainment, movies, music, TV, boyfriends, girlfriends, or anything other than God, you are just setting yourself up for a painful fall. I encourage you to seek a strong relationship with God before anything else. You may not always get the answers you want from God, but you must trust that He has your best interest in mind. For example, I didn't want my relationship with my fiancé to end, but it turned out to be the best thing that ever happened to me. God positively changed my life forever and helped me find true happiness after that.

Getting to know God requires relentless effort. Expect it to be difficult. It may take a long time to begin to understand how He is speaking to you. It actually took me four years of relentless effort and daily journaling before I finally recognized how God was trying to communicate with me.

Through my experiences, I discovered that one of the key components of prayer is learning how to *listen*. Sometimes you need to make your prayer request and then wait for an answer. You could get an answer right away, but be prepared for it to take years to finally understand what God is saying. Prepare yourself to spend every moment of every day listening.

If you think God has given you an answer, write it down and test it. Wait to see what the outcome is. Did it turn out the way you expected or not? Were you correct in what you thought God was telling you or not? Make careful note of the thoughts and feelings you experienced. One of the biggest challenges of listening in prayer is learning how to tell the difference between God's voice and your own wishful thinking. Over time you will begin to recognize the subtle differences in your thoughts and feelings when God is authentically speaking to you and when He is not.

As you seek to develop your relationship with God, keep in mind that we are made in His image and likeness. He is very caring, understanding, and down to earth. He has the ability to be happy, joyful, and even playful at times. He can also get emotionally upset, annoyed, and angry with us. I know from personal experience that I can actually piss God off! He was authentically mad at me for having sex with Nancy at the end of my senior year of high school, and I actually felt His anger. Although I didn't know it at the time, I was hurting myself which in turn upset God. I hope you will choose to avoid making the same mistakes I made. I hope you want to make God happy rather than upset Him.

Even if you hurt God, He isn't going to hold it against you. He's not like us in that way. He doesn't hold a grudge. Even when He is upset, He wants to forgive us and embrace us. Sometimes the hardest part about sinning is forgiving ourselves after we've done something wrong. If you ever make a big mistake like I have, just remember how much God was there for me, especially when I needed Him the most! He is just as much there for you too. The most important discipline you can ever develop is to go to God with everything that happens in your life, even if you've done something horribly wrong. The worst thing you could ever possibly do is stay away from God.

In addition to praying on your own, I strongly recommend getting involved with prayer groups and Church groups. They provide positive support, and they encourage you to live the right way. I'm sure you could see from my experiences that sharing your life with people who truly believe in God is much better than living without them! Also, when you go to Church, *give it your best effort*! You *need* to overcome your fear of what other people think and put your whole heart into the songs, prayers, and responses! If you do, you *will feel peace* and you *will feel God*. If you don't, then you will walk away as if nothing ever happened.

I hope this conclusion section has helped put a few of the key ideas of this book into perspective for you. I really encourage you to keep *I've Got To Change* as a reference and resource as you go through life. As you mature, go back and reread this story. You will probably begin to notice many subtle messages and hidden lessons I provided but didn't deliberately point out to you. To convey these messages, I carefully chose every word and every detail as I recounted each situation.

In order to find every hidden lesson, you will need to pay acute attention to detail and analyze the thoughts and words I used. Sometimes you will also need to recognize the implied details in order to catch the full message. For example, check out the very beginning of the book where Brent and I snuck out of his house to go back to the party. Watch all of my thoughts and actions carefully. You will probably notice that all of my decisions were rooted in my insecurity and desire to be liked. The first wrong decision I made was to let Brent talk me into sneaking out of his house to go back to the party. I should have just said *no* to him. I was afraid to do that because I was trying to get him to like me as a friend. As a result, I did what he wanted. Have you ever done that? It is *not* a good idea. In my case, it was my first step down the path of disaster! Then, while we were at the party, and there was a threat of cops showing up, I should have said, "We are leaving now!" Instead, I acted insecurely again and let him have his way. Next, I allowed Todd to talk me into letting him drive us back to the party. I didn't want to get in the car with him. I was afraid of confrontation and other people's opinion, so I gave in to his persistence. The hidden message in that whole section is that you *need* to learn how to recognize your inner fears and weaknesses and then overcome them by forcing yourself to make the right decision. *If you do not **force yourself** to have assertive courage, but allow other people and insecure emotions to control your life, then you will end up hurt in some way.* In my case, I almost got killed. Just remember that the choice is yours to make, and you should expect it to be difficult!

As you reread my story looking for these hidden lessons, it may be a good idea to have a notepad handy to make a list of all the important lessons you notice. You can also use the blank pages I provided for you at the very end of this book. Having a list of ideas on paper makes it easier to create a game plan for applying them to your life and tracking the results. You can also compare notes with friends to see if they noticed something you didn't.

With that in mind, I ask you to help me spread my message by recommending this book to as many people as possible. If someone gave you this book, maybe you could thank them for it and encourage them to keep giving it to people. I'd also really appreciate it if you wrote some positive reviews for it on the Internet. Please keep in mind that I *need* your support and help in getting people to read my story.

I could conclude this book with a real inspiring discourse in an attempt to motivate you to change your life in a positive way. Rather than do that, I'd like you to slowly and calmly make a definitive choice to embark on a long path that will take time and effort. I don't want you to make a decision based solely on emotion but on common sense and a firm resolve to constantly work at positively changing as a person throughout your entire life. Don't rely on emotions to motivate you to make this decision. Your emotions will come and go. As you apply all the concepts you've learned in this book, be patient with yourself, and give yourself time to develop. Always remember how patient God was with me and how I didn't change everything all at once. I changed one major thing at a time and then moved on to the next one. At times, I had to go back and work on something that I thought I had already fixed.

Although there are many valuable lessons contained in these pages, there is much more I want to share with you, so I hope you will read the other books I've written. For now, I encourage you to stay focused on all the ways that *you've got to change*. Keep asking yourself, "If I would have died today, would I have gone to heaven?" May God bless you in your efforts!

EPILOGUE—About this book and others I have written

As I write these words, it has been about seventeen years since the car accident and around thirteen years since I had my encounter with God that made me realize, "I've got to change!" I never intended to write a book about myself like this. It all started when I wrote about the evangelization missionary experiences I had after college. I gave a copy of them to my family members hoping it would inspire them to become more vocal about their faith and motivate them to grow closer to God.

They all loved reading my stories. My Grandmother liked them so much that she asked me to write more. This surprised me, and I simply didn't know what else to say. At the same time, I had a growing desire to get more people to read about my missionary experiences. I hoped that every reader would feel inspired to live their faith more actively and courageously. I also hoped that non-Catholics would want to become Catholic.

My solution was to write about my car accident to use as an attention getter and put it in front of the missionary experiences. After working on it for about two months, my life circumstances forced me to put the whole project on the shelf where it sat collecting dust for several years. When I was finally able to start working on it again, I realized it was missing the middle of the story. The book started with the car accident when I was seventeen and then jumped to the street evangelization missions I went on at the age of twenty-three.

It took me a year to fill in the middle details and figure out what to call this book. Let me tell you, that was a tough year! It was not easy coming face to face with all the sins of my past and admitting them to everyone. It helped me realize just how much of a sinner I have been and how much I need Jesus to save me. It also helped me be much friendlier and non-preachy in my approach to call other people to conversion. I hope that the way I have shared my story will enable the Holy Spirit to reach right through the pages of my life and touch the heart of every reader.

Once my whole story was on paper, I realized that the encounter I had with God after my cousin died, and my fiancé dumped me, was the pivotal changing moment of my entire life. Without that experience, I may never have changed my ways. That monumental moment left me yelling at the top of my lungs, "I've got to change!" Realizing this made it clear that *I've Got To Change* was the appropriate title for this book.

In the process, I realized that *I've Got To Change* had mysteriously evolved into something I had never intended it to be. The focus was no longer on the missionary experiences. It had actually become a modern day book on repentance and an experiential handbook on morality. The message of this book is very much what John the Baptist called people to do in preparation for the coming of the Messiah. REPENT, or should I say CHANGE, "For the Kingdom of God is at hand!"

To streamline this message, I took the missionary experiences out of this book and developed them into a separate book which I have titled *Will You Spread My Word For Me?* I hope you will consider reading it, especially if you have questions about the Catholic Church and its teachings. *Will You Spread My Word For Me?* will be particularly helpful if you are still trying to find your religious foundation. Having a religious foundation is utterly important as you grow and develop as a person because it provides a moral framework for making good decisions. Without it, you run the risk of being tossed around by the turbulent winds of the world and possibly ending up shipwrecked.

To help people avoid getting "shipwrecked" I am planning to write a book on self-knowledge and self-awareness. It will explain the inner workings of a human being and various things that can influence our choices. You may find that knowledge helpful in addition to all that you have learned through this book.

In addition to making good decisions in your everyday life, it is very important to make the right decision about your vocation. While I was growing up, I formulated my own plans for my future without ever asking God what His plan was for my life. As my love for God grew, so did my desire to do His will instead of my own. I started to ask Him what vocation He was calling me to. There was a major dilemma that became painfully clear to me when I started to ask God this question. I didn't know how to listen to Him or how He would communicate His answer to me. Choosing right from wrong in order to *change* was much easier because it was written out in His commandments and could be followed. Hearing God's calling for my life was something spiritual and had to be discerned.

I immediately found the process of discernment utterly confusing and overwhelmingly difficult. Nothing seemed clear, and I kept questioning, "How do you find God's will for your life? How do you know for sure what you are supposed to do? Who or what are you supposed to listen to in making this decision?" My intense desire to fulfill God's plan for my life, coupled with my human insecurities, left me feeling very afraid of making the wrong vocational choice. To make matters worse, even the people who were supposed to be directing me seemed to be twisting me in knots. My whole discernment process ended up taking *four **agonizing long years*** before I finally realized what God had been saying to me all along. In fact, it was because I was going through this difficult discernment process that the original version of *I've Got To Change* "sat on the shelf collecting dust" all those years.

Although I had a terrible time trying to see my own vocation clearly during much of the discernment process, I was able see firsthand that many other people were committing themselves to the WRONG VOCATION! Some were called to the religious life or the priesthood but were getting married. Others were called to marriage but were joining the priesthood or a religious order. Some were called to marriage but were marrying the wrong person. WHAT A MESS! This is tragic, not just for the individual, but for the rest of the world! *No one else* on earth can fulfill God's plan for your life the way you can! That is why it is so important for you to be where God intends you to be and doing what He created you to do!

I recorded my experiences and some of the key lessons I learned about discernment in the sequel to *I've Got To Change*, which is titled *What's My Vocation?* Chronologically, *What's My Vocation?* begins just after the section in this book titled "Jesus, If

That's You, Prove It." Knowing this will help you to see the overlapping events between *What's My Vocation?* and *I've Got To Change.*

I believe *What's My Vocation?* will not only help you find your true calling in life, but it will help you find it with a lot less pain and suffering than I had to endure! It will provide you with examples and ideas of how to listen for God in your everyday experiences, so I strongly encourage you to read it!

ABOUT THE AUTHOR

Sean McVeigh was raised in a small rural town in Pennsylvania. His main hobbies, interests, and activities have been archery, fishing, hiking, hunting, camping, basketball, baseball, snowboarding, skateboarding, writing books and magazine articles, playing the guitar, and writing music. He seeks to live a fulfilling life and help others find true happiness. His writing and guest speaking style are simple, realistic, down to earth, attractive, and inspiring! Many people have greatly benefited from Sean's influence. Are you one of them?

www.ingramcontent.com/pod-product-compliance
Lightning Source LLC
Chambersburg PA
CBHW072337300426
44109CB00042B/1663